THE ANGEL
OF THE
LAW OF ATTRACTION

4 in 1

A Sacred Guide to Understanding and Manifest Money, Love, Success, and Health in Our Lives

Bonus: *The New Secrets to Winning the Lottery*

Containing 4 books from the series: A voice from Quiet

ISABEL TOHEN

Text Copyright © Isabel Tohen

All rights reserved.

No part of this guide may be reproduced in any form without permission in writing from the publisher except in the case of brief quotations embodied in critical articles or reviews.

Legal & Disclaimer

The information contained in this book and its contents is not designed to replace or take the place of any form of medical or professional advice; and is not meant to replace the need for independent medical, financial, legal or other professional advice or services, as may be required. The content and information in this book has been provided for educational and entertainment purposes only.

The content and information contained in this book has been compiled from sources deemed reliable, and it is accurate to the best of the Author's knowledge, information and belief. However, the Author cannot guarantee its accuracy and validity and cannot be held liable for any errors and/or omissions. Further, changes are periodically made to this book as and when needed. Where appropriate and/or necessary, you must consult a professional (including but not limited to your doctor, attorney, financial advisor or such other professional advisor) before using any of the suggested remedies, techniques, or information in this book.

Upon using the contents and information contained in this book, you agree to hold harmless the Author from and against any damages, costs, and expenses, including any legal fees potentially resulting from the application of any of the information provided by this book. This disclaimer applies to any loss, damages or injury caused by the use and application, whether directly or indirectly, of any advice or information presented, whether for breach of contract, tort, negligence, personal injury, criminal intent, or under any other cause of action.

You agree to accept all risks of using the information presented inside this book.

You agree that by continuing to read this book, where appropriate and/or necessary, you shall consult a professional (including but not limited to your doctor, attorney, or financial advisor or such other advisor as needed) before using any of the suggested remedies, techniques, or information in this book.

Table of Contents

Introduction to the Collection 9

The Angel of the Law of Attraction: How to Attract Money and Prosperity. The Secret of Wealth and Everything You Need to Know to Develop Your Skills to Manifest Money 13

Preface 13

Chapter 1: Angels Guide Us Towards Prosperity 15

Chapter 2: Demanding 19

Chapter 3: Faith and Gratitude 23

Chapter 4: The 6 Steps of Power 27

Chapter 5: The Mirror Law 33

Chapter 6: Winning the Lottery with the Law of Attraction 35
    Decide the Amount to Win 37
    Steps to Mental Rescheduling and Developing the Attitude to Wealth 39
    When to Use These Powerful Statements? 41
    Powerful Statements to Win the Lottery 42

Final Remarks 45

The Angel of the Law of Attraction: The Practical Exercises to Develop Your Skills to Quickly Manifest Money, Success and Prosperity 47

Preface 47

Chapter 1: Shaping, Cleaning, and Marking 51

Chapter 2: The 5 Physical/ Mental Rescheduling Techniques of Alignment with the Intentions of Soul Prosperity 55

Chapter 3: The Virtual Tattoo 59

Chapter 4: Satisfaction of Your Life 61

Chapter 5: Light Charity 65

Chapter 6: Allowing and Receiving: Opening the Golden Door 67

Chapter 7: Acceptance and Gratitude 71

Final Remarks 73

The Angel of the Law of Attraction: The Secret to Happy Relationships by Developing Your Abilities to Receive Friendship, Kindness and Love 75

Preface 75

Chapter 1: Remembering Myself 79

Chapter 2: Shed Light in Yourself 83

Chapter 3: Unconditional Love and Possession 87

Chapter 4: Your Soulmate Really Exists: You Are Already Connected and You Do Not Know It 91

Chapter 5: Recognizing and Choosing Each Other: The Beginning of the Journey Together 95

Chapter 6: Think of the Best Version of Yourself and Make It Happen 97

Final Remarks 101

The Angel of the Law of Attraction: The Secret to Constantly Manifest Wellness and Health in Your Life 103

Preface 103

Chapter 1: We Attract Illness Just Like the Other Experiences 107

Chapter 2: Acceptance or Resignation 111

Chapter 3: Suffering in the Healing Process 115

Chapter 4: Health and Wellness as a Choice 119

Chapter 5: All-Around Therapies 123

Chapter 6: Love, Gratitude, and Forgiveness 127
Final Remarks 131
Conclusion to the Collection 135

This work comes from loving

Invitation from my husband to carry out

And make it manifest in this life

My essence,

And doing what I feel I was born for.

And with Love I do it.

To Giada, Alessandro, Benedetta and Miriam

They improve the world and my life with their

Existence

And to my Angel...

Heartfelt thanks

Introduction to the Collection

***Wealth is like sea-water:
the more we drink,
the thirstier we become.***

Arthur Schopenhauer

The first thing I have joyfully learned from my Guardian Angel is that we are entitled to prosperity and wealth in our lives.

Everybody, without exceptions.

The second thing I had to accept and fully understand with dismay is that if we live an unsatisfying and poor life, the responsibility is ours alone.

There is no one to blame out there, but the only thing to do is to roll up your sleeves if you decide to understand the way things are.

However, this is our choice, and no one in heaven or on Earth can force us to be happy, rich, and satisfied until this truth gets through our heads and hearts; poverty is a disease, and it must be treated as one.

The lack of abundance is neither necessary nor formative if it is not considered only temporary and used as a spur, as a strong motivation to seek the truth of things.

In this journey you are going to take, you will learn to bring wealth, money, love, and health into your life, day by day and with more and more joy, because you will be accompanied with love by someone who, since the beginning of time, has been made available to men to give help and support.

But don't expect a Godsend without doing anything.

This is not the aim.

You will be led and properly educated to become consciously the creators of your reality; you will not find hidden treasures, but you will learn to create your wealth and your freedom from the need every day.

For this reason, besides guiding you step by step on an inner journey in self-discovery, mental functioning, its traps, and heart-opening, you will be taught practical exercises to shape with the fire of the will (sadly, without it, you can do very little) the new feeling, the new vision that will be the basis of the new life that you will be called to live.

You will challenge yourself, your beliefs will crumble in the face of the evidence of what has never worked, and finally, you will have a rich and prosperous life.

All the lies will be disclosed, one by one.

You will get familiar with the Law of Attraction, to understand its functioning, and above all, to recognize its hints in every aspect of your daily life, thus becoming your dearest and closest friend, from which gain information and support for everything you want to manifest in your reality.

You will also learn the importance of contact with your subconscious, lord and master of events that happen whether we wanted them on a conscious level or not, where all the psychological mechanisms and beliefs are rooted, piled up there in years, and that condition all existence.

You will have the answers to the questions:

1. What is stopping me from living a rich and prosperous life?
2. Why do I always have little money to do what makes me happy?
3. How can I be successful?
4. Why don't I have love in my life?
5. Why do I lack health?

You have tried for many years to understand the reason why you are living this way; you have tried to change your way of thinking and to condition your mind with propositional words and phrases, but almost nothing has changed and you are left with mere great frustration.

I know all these feelings, I have felt them on my skin and in my heart.

At first, I tried to use only the strength of my thought and my mind as well to create the life I wanted, but I failed miserably.

I had no idea that I was manifesting the reality of my deep convictions, rooted since my birth, and of all my negative feelings that gradually set more and more.

Don't be fooled by your mind; the painful and negative past experiences you think you have overcome are still there, hidden like shadows that must be brought to light, heard, to be dissolved once and for all.

I learned to do it thanks to my Angel, the guide of a voice that comes from the quiet.

Every minute of every day.

This is how I accomplished my journey: opening my eyes and observing, constantly, everything I did not like and caused me grief, without blaming the outer world or complaining, but going back inside me, again and again.

I didn't just want to understand, I wanted to be FREE!

In the end, I won.

So understanding came.

This is my gift to you.
The rest is in your hands and in your heart.

The Angel of the Law of Attraction: How to Attract Money and Prosperity. The Secret of Wealth and Everything You Need to Know to Develop Your Skills to Manifest Money

Preface

"Life is the first gift, love is the second

and understanding, the third."

Marge Pierce

There is a deep need for knowledge in every man and woman's heart, which can be summed up in a question: Why?

Why do I exist, why am I here, why this family, why this body, why this economic situation, why this sentimental situation, and still, why do I live in this health condition? Why can't I make my dreams come true, why so much unhappiness... why, why, why?

The usefulness and, therefore, the necessity of this –quick reference handbook– is mainly in the interview setting, a conversation during which through my research, with peaks of stinging suffering, years and years of doubts and uncertainties melt and were desperately looking for answers.

The effort, I admit, was mostly from my interlocutor; that is, making his answers quickly comprehensible not only to me but also to those who, in the future, wanted to benefit from them.

Guides have always been made available to humankind, however, our spiritual and mental evolution was so limited that only a select group of chosen ones held the answers to the secrets of existence. The truth is today available and comprehensible to all, only if we dare to go beyond the limits of what appears to our physical senses, and let the heart finally open and the consciousness expands, day by day, becoming the masters of ourselves.

In this light, the topics debated over the years have been many and all lead gradually to an ever higher and fuller knowledge of the reasons of life and of how it works, of the laws that regulate it, and of why we struggle to apply consciously such laws.

In this journey, I was taken by the hand and led, slowly, out of the tunnel of failures, from doubts, from limiting beliefs. I "cleaned up" myself of everything I did not want in my life, and that represented the main obstacles to the realization of my real desires.

I realized I personally was the creator of my successes and failures, I learned and I still do it, not to live in fear and guilt and to choose love, forgiveness, and gratitude

This is what I call wellbeing and this is what I wish for each of you too.

Chapter 1: Angels Guide Us Towards Prosperity

"True prosperity does not come from the abundance of material goods,

but from a peaceful mind."

Mohammed

The Guardian Angel is a wonderful gift that fully expresses the Creator's love for each creature and child.

All of us can communicate with our guardian angel, even if not in a conscious way, listening, grasping the synchronicities, and following the insights generated not by our mind but rather our heart.

Angels are constantly close to us and in touch with us, at least with our

Higher Self, even if sadly, our limited mind is not always able to grasp the signs that our protectors continually send us.

Especially in some moments of our life when things are not going right and we feel crushed by life.

There is a lack of faith in everything and everyone and what we cannot do is relying on who knows what is best for us.

Only in some rare cases what is best for us corresponds to pain, sadness, and sacrifice; most of the time, this negative state of affairs is our unconscious choice to split the hardness of our mind clung only to what knows and believes the right way is.

The mind, most of the time, lies when it is not enlightened by deep insights that come from our soul.

In short, that's the way it is, get over it; in this world, we suffer, even a lot, unless we take a path of inner contact by letting ourselves be helped by those who have been placed close to us on purpose with this exact task and mission.

The Guardian Angel is always there for us every time we need Him or that we just want to have a chat with a true friend, or to feel that love that comes from the Creator, and that only limiting and negative thoughts can keep away from us.

If you ask me, I have always spoken with the Voice (at first I used to call it that), sometimes calmly, sometimes (most of the time) with anger, hatred, sadness, and absolute victimhood.

I always thought I was right, always.

It was not like this!

Why would I talk to him? God only knows. The fact is that my questions did not amaze me as much as the answers or the claims on these issues left me astonished.

I would not have got those answers for sure.

So which side of my mind did they come from?

Nowhere.

It took me years to understand that my mind had nothing to do with it.

The topics covered in these long conversations were several, some very private, others instead ranged from work, health, relationship problems, and for a certain (hard) period, even money.

Over the years, I got into the habit of jotting down some important transitions of these conversations, and recently I had the idea of sharing what seems to me to have been a – gift –, a self-listening skill (I do not know how to call it), gathering this work in small handbooks of reflection on life's hardness and beauty.

I started to give the benefit to what I was told, verifying from time to time, with practical feedback, advice, and suggestions to solve thorny situations in my life.

I verified by experience that to hear the voice clearly, I had to be in a situation of mental calm because in chaotic moments, I could not perceive it.

It wasn't easy at all.

However, the aids and the miracles I have seen happen in my life, the well-being brought to everyone, have confirmed me from time to time, the loving source of this Voice.

I began to trust in my Guardian Angel both during the day (when I was more or less connected with Him) and during the night through the dreams originated from that special source.

I slowly began to feel his embrace and loving touch full of grace and acceptance, with deep faith and gratitude.

I was ready to listen to everything, to say what had to be said without sparing anything, in a sort of restorative silence.

I had no idea how important silence was.

I have unclear memories of when I began to talk sporadically with her, the quiet voice, but I know that one day I realized that she was there.

It was not gradual, I would call it a flash, with a bang, that's it.

Then everything happened.

At Her suggestion, I decided to write some small easy-to-use handbooks, and not a book full of all the topics (which are really a lot) dealt with the Angel, to make it easier in some areas, helping you to solve the problems that distress us the most.

However, I warn you; no one, in Heaven and on Earth, will do the work for you, so without tenacity and faith you will not go anywhere, with or without the precious help of your Angel.

This is not about magic, but about an awareness growth path using aids that we did not hope to have.

So this first handbook will help you bring prosperity, abundance, and wealth into your life. Warning: I'm not promising that after reading this book you will become John Davison Rockefeller, but that each of us will have according to what – he will give – and what he needs to fulfill his goal.

Here are some tips to receive help from the angels.

Chapter 2: Demanding

"Grab someone's hand who will help you,

and then use it to help someone else. "

Booker T. Washington

One of the great gifts of the Creator to men is the free will law. Only we decide whether to get help or not; free will is sacred!

It is, therefore, necessary for our will to ask for divine intervention, otherwise, as a result of this law, the angels cannot help us.

It is usually our Guardian Angel who takes charge of everything concerning us, and even though we all know that angelic hierarchies exist, He is the closest to us, and His vibration is more similar (let me use the term) to ours, so it is easier for us to communicate and receive messages and help, or an answer can come through a prayer addressed to the Angels or simply saying "Help me."

I was very reticent to deal with issues concerning money, prosperity, and wealth in general, they seemed to me to be too --human-- topics. On the other hand, all religions encourage the seeking of spiritual rather than material wealth. So when I asked, in a moment of discouragement, why the Creator allowed all this poverty in the world and why there were continually economic problems in my life too, the answer was simple and surprising at the same time.

Guardian Angel, "If you had children, what would you like for them, that they always lived without problems in a constant state of well-being and economic wealth donated by you, parent, or would you prefer them to learn through aids and teachings, experiences, perhaps not always pleasant, to *create* by themselves wealth and prosperity so that no one could force them to live in poverty anymore? Everything that happens in your life, every time you ask for prosperity and wealth from the Universe, is necessary so that those qualities useful to attract by Resonance what is asked take root in you; Abundance, Prosperity, and Wealth. Only after the inner change takes place, the outer change can manifest itself in reality. In this way, the Law of Attraction acts.

It is never the contrary.

You chose a long time ago to leave Eden to learn to create the reality you want yourself, but you always blame the Father who does not provide for you. The choice has always been yours since the beginning of time, but that doesn't mean you have been left alone."

Me, "Do you think so? I see too much loneliness in the world.

Even now I feel lonely and tired.

If every human being has a Guardian Angel next to them, why is there all this pain then?

You Angels, perhaps, talk to too few people ..."

G.A, "The point is not who or how many people we talk to; everyone hears, but very few people choose to listen to us. And this is also your free will.

You will feel overcome with poverty until you have had enough. You might be surprised by the human's resistance. You have a strange relationship with money even today, you yearn for it, and at the same time, you despise it. You live and are even willing to die for it. You should make a decision and choose once and for all how you want to relate to the concept of wealth, actually. As long as you think you *own* wealth, it will always run away, when you change your mind about using wealth, it will become your friend, and it will come with you both in this and the next lives you will live on Earth. Money is like energy; it must be moving, it renews itself, and it must necessarily flow; stop clinging to it and thinking the more you have, the safer you are. Stop being afraid and use the energy you waste worrying and doubting, instead, to convert it into the energy of gratitude."

But why? Wasn't I grateful...?

Not really, I took for granted what I had and demanded what I didn't have.

I forgot I was grateful, I was more used to being angry and frustrated, and from morning to night, there was always a hidden discouragement and victimhood in me.

Oh God, how horrible! How did I become like this, why did I allow it?

However, I still thought I had good reasons.

ME, "It's hard to be grateful when you can't make ends meet, or when you can never buy what you like, and every month you have to give away even personal gratifications. I know that compared to the tragic situations they tell on the news maybe I'm not doing that bad, but I still feel frustrated, stuck in a sort of time loop in which the days are, more or less, always the same. Here, I'm tired! I would like to be free from economic problems once and for all, but I have no idea how to do it."

G.A, "Complaining is not the right way for sure, but you really like it, or more precisely, your mind likes it. Think about it; the complaint, the worry, the doubt, the frustration, the anger, what did they produce, or better, what did they bring you? I will tell you; another complaint, other worries, other doubts, other frustration... this is the time loop you were talking about, isn't it?

Actually, they are feelings that come from the ungratefulness for everything that is already there in your life. Try to think about it; everything in your life exists thanks to your act of gratitude, you might not remember it now, but that's it. When something or someone is no longer part of your life (despite yourself), it is because you have started to take it for granted, to be ungrateful. When something or someone enters your life and you are happy with it, it happens mainly because of an act of gratitude, perhaps not for the event itself, but certainly for something linked to the occurred event.

How grateful are you for all the good things you have now?"

ME, "The secret to fulfill our abundance and prosperity desires is being just grateful? That's it?"

Chapter 3: Faith and Gratitude

They asked, "What's the best thing to own?"

Buddha answered,

"Faith is the best thing you can have."

G.A, "That's it? If there were an extra drop of gratitude in every men's heart, mountains would move."

ME, "Isn't faith that moves mountains?"

G.A, "There is no true gratitude without faith."

ME, "I ask with my prayers for what I want to achieve, I try to have faith thinking that what I want has already appeared, trying to feel good, like those who teach the Law of Attraction, but no matter how hard I try, I can't, nothing happens. I can't control anything. I just can't do it, and I do not know why.

G.A, "You will not get what you want because in your prayer there is the heartfelt statement of what you lack, such as money, and all your attention and your feelings are focused on the lack in your life. The fulfilling prayer is never a request, but gratitude."

ME, "But if what I want a life *free from need, rich, and prosperous* despite my gratitude, does not manifest itself, I would be deeply disappointed and embittered. I know, it has already happened to me several times."

G.A, "I see, you have not solved your financial problems yet. But I know that other things were given to you almost before you asked for them many times. But we will get back to this part.

Gratitude is not a bargaining chip, the laws of the Universe cannot be manipulated.

Much less making fun of yourself. If you say thank you for something you perfectly know does not exist in your real life, why don't you think the Universe is aware of this at least as much as you are? You and the Universe are not two separate realities, even if this illusion takes over the minds of men. What you know matches perfectly with the Universe's knowledge, and it is the perfect expression of your reality.

That is why faith and gratitude cannot be separated; what is declared existing because You say so in the name of the divine being in you, all the holiness of the Universe is required to act and to reveal your will. Faith and devotion's intensity behind each thankful prayer is directly proportional to the speed of manifestation in reality.

This is why the amazement for the Law of Attraction turns into disappointment and incredulity soon. The Law always works whether you are aware of it or not; this era's challenge is being able to process it in the right way through the three bodies of men –physical, emotional, and mental– in this way, you will win one of the hardest battles for the human race –the one against poverty and deprivation–; but as long as most of your life is devoted to material survival, there will always be little room and time to devote to what really matters to you, to your development."

ME, "When you say Universe, do you mean God? After all, it is all up to Him..."

G.A, "If you want, I can replace God with Universe, it really doesn't make any difference. But the question is 'Who decides what?'

Requests to be fulfilled or not?

Why on earth do you imagine such a weird God?

You were created to His image and likeness and given free will; why give you something and then take it back?

The power of creation has always been hidden where you would never have reached deep down; within you.

It is about time to rediscover and use it accurately and consciously. It's not difficult, it's just challenging."

The days after the discussion with my Angel were challenging from many points of view. However, the growing awareness of my power made me strangely quieter. I was somehow less likely to gripes, doubts, and the constant mood swings that usually exhausted me during the day.

I was, like, the best version of myself.

I didn't know it yet, but the power of "I Am" was already at work, and I was also verifying The Law of the Mirror, all truths that turned my lifetime upside-down for the better.

I had begun to be fully responsible for my life and I was terrified. I didn't know how to act, but I couldn't go back; the journey had begun.

Oddly, my co-workers were the first to notice this change; however, they did not report it to me in words, but with their behavior; they were more solicitous and careful towards me, almost intrigued, and this thing amused and amazed me. A colleague of mine even asked me if I got botox on my face...

My answer was obviously no, but I doubt she believed me.

However, the state of harmony and inner stillness began to manifest itself externally, but I had no eyes to see.

Not yet.

There were many questions about the Law of Attraction, but above all, I wanted to put it into practice, I wanted to start using it consciously and I didn't want to fail this time.

I had really had enough of collecting defeats.

So that evening, after an intense but satisfying working day, I was looking forward to facing this topic with my Guardian Angel. I wanted to start practicing as we kept going with the theory. So I asked without hesitation, "Is there a way fast enough to learn to put the Law of Attraction into practice with awareness?"

G.A, "Theory is never separated from practice.

When the mind focuses on certain topics for a certain period of time, it causes new synapses in the brain, it essentially changes the way nerve cells communicate with each other (neurons) or with other cells. This is to say that when the way of thinking and the topics change, everything starts to change, inside and out.

To start mastering the Law of Attraction and manifesting the desired experiences in this three-dimensional reality, you need to proceed step by step.

I know it would be more pleasant doing some simple physical and mental exercises, but it is not like a foreign language or painting course.

Especially since the mind could be the biggest limit.

It has been said several times in the past 'The spirit is willing, but the flesh is weak.'"

ME, "In fact ...I realized that when I want something, something material I mean, I am a bit ashamed, as if desiring material wealth or prosperity is less worthy than wishing to develop virtues, such as compassion, altruism or generosity. I just feel so, and I am angry about it because I am not going anywhere."

G.A, "I totally get it, and I know your heart. However, I ask you, who craves virtue and noble sentiments, peace in the world, food, and care for all living beings, not feeling guilty, can always manifest his desires in this reality?"

ME, "Well, I do not think so..."

G.A, "So, the key to realization is another. An effort of will alone, no matter how great, is therefore not enough.

That is why I will help you focus on the essential waypoints to use the Law of Attraction.

But we must start from the beginning. The first step is: **just remember who you are and whose daughter you are.**"

Chapter 4: The 6 Steps of Power

"We know that no one ever seizes power with the intention of relinquishing it."
George Orwell

The hardest thing in writing this handbook was to make the content of the dialogues with my Angel immediate and usable, carefully choosing from notes and memories felt when, gradually, the fog concerning the problems in my life cleared.

I was completely wrong about what to do to and achieve one's goals. In fact, there was very little to do, especially at the beginning. We had to turn our attention to our inner reality, to which we usually spend little time, rather than the external one.

After the last dialogue with my Guardian Angel, I decided to think alone about his last words "Remember who you are and whose daughter you are." No matter how obvious they might seem, they had had an unexpected impact on me; they shifted my attention towards my true origin, not human, but spiritual.

In the end, I decided to ask, "Well, if I got this right, I will never go anywhere until I have clear my nature? Would every effort be vain and the results shallow? "

G.A, "Assuming you can somehow get results. Anyway yes, that's it! If you are not aware of yourself, you have no real power. By virtue of your origins, you are entitled to a rich and prosperous life. Start taking over this right in your heart. That is why this is the first and fundamental step to start the understanding work of the Law of Resonance, or Attraction. Your divine origin is what allows the conscious use of this Law.

But let's move on.

The second step is asking **with Gratitude and Faith**, eliminating judgment."

We are judging beings; every minute, every moment of our life we deliver a sentence, towards us and/or towards others.

We judge things, events, and people all the time, without noticing it, automatically.

And quitting is really hard.

G.A, "Eliminating judgment is not impossible, it is, as I said before, mainly challenging. It is an attention and observation work of the automatic mechanisms in which the human mind is continuously absorbed. If you wish abundance and prosperity in your life, this desire is immediately sabotaged by judgment and selfishness. You are the one blaming yourself and thwarting the expression of material wealth in your reality. As if God or the Universe had explicitly asked you to live in poverty to be considered beloved sons and worthy of love. It has never been like this, despite your beliefs."

ME, "So, eliminating the judgment on our desire to live in abundance, our request is already soaked with Gratitude and Faith. Without judgment, the feeling of Gratitude and Faith is automatically strengthened."

G.A, "Exactly. And like anything else, constant attention and observation can produce long-term effects. Let's go on, there is still a lot to say.

The third step is **Forgiveness**."

If eliminating judgment seemed to be a titanic challenge, I had always considered forgiveness to be for the chosen few.

G.A, "Many things have been said about forgiveness too, entire books, and long lectures, which, I see, have been of little use. Forgiveness in itself does not exist and would not make much sense if you do not open your heart first, and this can only happen through Love and Compassion.

Don't be afraid, I know that this process develops over entire lifetimes, and you don't need to become enlightened Masters to bring material well-being into your current existence.

However, this inner work must begin immediately and with constant effort, day by day. Only then, with the *burning* chest, you can elevate Love in Forgiveness, towards you, others, and any kind of lived experience. You will actually feel the flame of forgiveness, love, and gratitude, right at the height of the solar plexus; and when it has finished burning, it will have changed the pain, anger, and loneliness weight into the gold of Love and Compassion."

We were only on the third step, and my mind was already spinning.

All this information was very difficult to process, although I recognized it as true.

The education I got was not close to this vision of life at all. I had grown up with the belief that to achieve results, I had to give something very important to me back, a sort of painful and angry barter with life. Actually, the only thing that we needed and worked, was to bring Presence and Love into my every action and thought. Over time, I would have gone through the choice between the vicious circle of the old education (which brought me minimal results, a lot of frustration, and little economic recognition) and the virtuous circle of the new vision (which already brought me the first practical results).

But I still had a long road ahead, and I absolutely wanted to root all this in me, to turn it into my new life reality.

G.A, "The fourth step is facing one's fear until it turns into Love.

The energies that move your thoughts and actions are two --Love and fear--. And most of the time, the second dominates you, perhaps through doubt, anger, envy, resentment, and so on. There is nothing else to say; it is required an act of courage before operating; face what scares you, including hard life, poverty, failure, and loneliness. It is useless to look the other way and silence them, because they will scupper every project, especially at the unconscious and subconscious level.

So yes, you would be doomed to failure."

As the days went by, I became more and more aware of how many demons were inside me in any shape; fearful thoughts about the future, events never overcome, and constant dissatisfaction with my present. I used to live like this every day and I was not aware of it. Until now.

My financial situation was just a reflection of how I was feeling... awful!

The first reaction to this new awareness was crying.

I could not stop crying, I felt all the misery of a life lived in fear, and I felt alone.

G.A, "You are not alone, you have never been. But I have no power over your choices. And if you choose to feel alone and to suffer, I will take it and wait until you have enough. My hand is always there to support you. I never leave you alone and without my Love."

Despite the alternation of effort and joy, I wanted to go on in this journey, and there were still two steps left, so after I recovered some peace, I asked my Angel to tell me about the fifth and sixth steps towards prosperity.

G.A, "The fifth step consists of cultivating the satisfaction of our daily life staying true to yourself; satisfaction helps to feed Gratitude and to indulge in the Universe confidently.

You must be like someone who starts building a house; he always has the finished work in mind and the joy of the final result in his heart, but he enjoys the process day by day. Brick by brick, he is fully satisfied with what he is doing in his present."

It has been a long time since I really felt satisfied with something. Days followed one after the other, more or less, all the same. I was waiting for something that wasn't there or that I didn't have. And consequently, I was neither happy nor satisfied. Never. All I could do was trying to disguise my discomfort for a job I didn't like for fear of running out of money, having bad relationships, being alone, and crowding my life with useless objects hoping to fill an unbridgeable void. Was it possible there was nothing that could give me real satisfaction in the present?

G.A, "Because you do not have eyes to see yet.

But you can try to use the Heart sight; review your days, your acquaintances without judging them, watch yourself like you are watching the great Love of your life. Do you see it? You already smile."

In fact, there was more than I thought.

It always took some time before the dialogues with my Guardian Angel resumed the interrupted thread of the 6 Steps towards economic Prosperity. We talked about other interesting topics concerning health, love relationships or relationships in general, the afterlife, reincarnation (some people still questioned the veracity about it; I suspect this thing amused him, not a little). I also started a series of practical exercises I called Shaping, Cleaning and Marking (**A.N** of practical exercises I will talk about in the following handbook), suggested by my Guide, which had the aim of strengthening everything we had talked about so that it remained sculpted in my head forever (not only to this existence).

Everything was impressed in my Consciousness.

The last step baffled me!

G.A, "The sixth and last step is Charity.

Whenever you earn money, give a part of it to charity, especially to those who do not even know you, possibly anonymously.

Charity makes abundance keep flowing into your life without blocking the flow of wealth, with the risk of falling back into the fear of lack and greed.

This act of help and generosity makes you *permeable* by making you go through the energetic flow of wealth and blessing you and others.

Like any other form of energy, wealth is not possessed, but it is used and managed in the best possible way.

On how much to give to charity, choose not only what is excessive to you, but try to offer a part of what you would have kept for yourself too.

Do your best in this regard."

Not that I was expecting anything in particular, but simply ... I never thought about how important this could be.

I was accustomed to giving to charity, but it was rich people stuff, what did this have to do with me?

But it was a matter of points of view; you do not give to Charity because you are rich, but you are rich because you give to Charity. Charity lays solid foundations for a future of Prosperity and Wealth for all.

Chapter 5: The Mirror Law

"Remember that life is like a mirror,

it smiles you if you look at it smiling"

Jim Morrison

While I was writing the 6 Steps of Power, I realized how my vision of the world and life was definitely changing, starting with my deeper and stronger attention.

I began to perceive (thanks to an objective vision) that there was nothing bad out there in the world or each human being (if not the choices and behaviors that each decides to adopt), and I sensed, although with some difficulty, that everything is already perfect as it is; everything brings us back to a deep presence and makes us understand the power we have to create the wonderful reality we desire.

However, some disturbing thoughts endured.

And I asked my Guardian Angel about that, "why, despite everything, in certain situations, do I feel annoyed towards things or people for no apparent reason? Why does it still seem wrong to me that some people live in wealth and others in poverty? Sometimes I struggle, despite everything, to see perfection in this reality."

G.A, "Only if you know how to wander into the deep of each of you, you will produce change.

The reality you see is just the faithful projection of what you are and think.

If you consider something beautiful, it is because the same beauty resides in you, and so it is for everything that causes you discomfort and annoyance too.

Everything is subjective, even if you have been taught the opposite.

You like something that another does not like, or you are bothered by something that another does not even perceive.

Get used to using external reality as a precious tool to know aspects of yourself that you didn't even know existed, and, above all, pay attention to the reactions that people, things, and events, for better or for worse, have caused in you because it means that have echoed with something that belongs to you.

The Law of Attraction can work wonders and lead you towards a life of abundance and prosperity, but it is also a sublime guide that demands constancy, commitment, and attention from its students.

So arm yourself with acceptance and honesty towards yourself and what you see manifested on the outside, especially if you don't like it; you have the power to change things and convert unease into joy for you and others.

And remember; the Law of the Mirror always applies."

Chapter 6: Winning the Lottery with the Law of Attraction

"When you resonate in harmony with every cell of your body, emotion, and thought, you start a dance that will put you in a state of constant beauty and inner well-being; your physiology changes, and everything becomes extraordinary inside and outside of you.

Therefore you can capture a quantum consciousness moment when you detach yourself from ordinary time and space.

And so you raise your brain frequencies."

Guardian Angel

I was very uncertain whether to write a chapter specifically about winning money through lotteries or not.

However, going on with this work and reading the hundreds of distress calls through e-mails, letters, or small meetings, I realized that it is important to talk about it.

But how?

How could I give exhaustive answers to make it clear that everything (even gambling money) must be seen as a continuous inside work for a rich, prosperous, and joyful life construction?

I have spoken many times with my Spiritual Guide about wealth, poverty, prosperity, money, and everything around these concepts.

And yet the frequent question is, "If the Law of Attraction exists, and it is always operative, why, despite my efforts and attempts, cannot I attract them through a lottery win? Nevertheless, every time I play my numbers, I have good intentions, positivity, and love. But, apparently, it is not enough! What am I doing wrong?

I happened to win small amounts at most, but not that large one that would change my life."

In short, I finally realized that people may also believe they can attract money through their work, daily commitment, but they still have great difficulty understanding that wealth can come from anywhere, in any form, and that this does not depend on luck (understood as meaningless).

And above all, for the law of attraction, nothing changes with manifesting 100 or 10 million dollars...

The limit to the amount of money, and the channel by which this money can come, is only in our minds and hearts.

So the key point was to make this delicate concept clear.

After a long line of conversations with my Spiritual Guide, I realized that even this winning lottery problem could be used as a great work on ourselves, to better understand what was eluding our conscious mind because it was hidden in our unconscious.

So, one day I asked a direct question to my Angel. I definitively wanted to be able to give complete answers and to help those who lived this situation with apprehension and sadness, thinking that winning the lottery was something beyond their control...

ME, "What is the best way to help people asking me for advice on how to win the lottery using the Law of Attraction?"

Guardian Angel, "In past ages, we have always inspired the minds of those who were inclined to receive our messages and directions. Many times we have been asked how to get rich, to create abundance and prosperity, but for only a few centuries, the question has increasingly focused on winning the lottery.

I have said over and over again that the Law of Attraction always works, it is always operative, whether you want to attract money through a job, an inheritance, or at gambling.

The whole process always starts from within, from the soul, the heart, and the mind of man or woman; when there is full inner alignment of these three parts, you are capable of properly formulating a request to the Universe so that you could become the creators of your reality.

This is what happens before someone wins the lottery.

However, it is also true that in 99.9% of cases, those who win an important amount do not even realize their inner state.

And that is why we attribute this victory to luck.

But luck (seen as a random event) has absolutely nothing to do with it."

I will keep saying that; chance does not exist, and who has eyes to see knows it.

If you had the possibility to analyze the Heart of a person who has just won the lottery, you would realize all the distress and constant work this person has lived and done in the past years, or even in his past lives...

And of course, as I mentioned before, few are aware of it and even fewer realize it.

If you truly want to be masters of your life, try to open your eyes and tune into the Truth.

It is now possible to use the energy of this deep change era and arrive at the quantum leap that will see the rise of a new Earth and an aware Humanity, including through the emotional and creative push of winning the lottery.

All life experiences lead to awakening, and this desire is no exception."

Decide the Amount to Win

Once you have decided the amount of money to receive, think about what you will do with it once you obtained it.

This work, seemingly only mental, is actually used to monitor everything that happens in your Heart; pay attention to your emotions in this delicate passage because you may discover unknown aspects of yourself.

For this reason, it is useful to tell Eliza's story, who after she wrote me several e-mails concerning winning the lottery, foresaw something really important about herself.

She wrote, "Dear Isabel, thank you for your help and support.

I want to tell you what happened to me when I started writing in a notebook (do you remember my personal wealth notebook?) what I would do if I had the amount of money I asked for.

From the very beginning, when I started the list, I felt a malicious discomfort insinuating into my soul.

I could not understand why, but the more I wrote, the more it increased until I decided to dig up inside myself to see clearly.

At first, I could not catch this biting discomfort because it sneaked out every time I tried to grab it, but in the end, backed into a corner, I did it, and I was astonished by what I saw.

My discomfort was made up of the pain of poverty years as a child and the degrading beliefs of my family, who considered money responsible for all evil in the world.

I could not believe that after so many years of psychotherapy, I still did not get over that phase of my life and remove all the limiting and false thoughts about wealth.

This thought was still rooted in my subconscious, although I was sure I eradicated it.

I was saddened but relieved at the same time; I now knew why I had never won a penny, and I knew (thanks to you) how to work on it and fix it as soon as possible.

I will never thank you enough for the *Light* you carried in my Heart."

This e-mail was a relief on a heavy day in which I found myself thinking about how many obstacles we are called to overcome every day.

I told my Spiritual Guide the emotion I felt reading this message and, as always, the answer went further, to the core of my discomfort.

Guardian Angel, "The hindering, slowing down, delaying forces… are the ones that, going against human's desire and plans, make them evolve endlessly.

Sickness, relationship, and money problems, as has been said, make you find out a new inner depth.

Everything that is reached quickly and effortlessly is not acquired on a deep level of awareness, while the friction due to discomfort allows this acquisition in the deepest levels of the soul.

You are not horses that life wants to drop, but rather train.

Sometimes a result takes long to appear just because you need a deeper level of inner transformation that only time and practice can bring.

Always remember that any distressful experience has a purpose, it is intentional; the obstacles on your path have been placed there by someone who knows more than your mind, *your Soul*.

Steps to Mental Rescheduling and Developing the Attitude to Wealth

Do not try persuading your mind or subconscious with simple positive statements about money, because they are not fooled by nice words.

So if you are not winning the lottery, it doesn't mean the Law of Attraction isn't working –it means you're giving contrasting and confusing vibrational signals, and this kind of disorganized energy is the result.

There is a need to look for the right method to reschedule the subconscious mind and also to check what and where the obstructions that block the installation of new beliefs are.

Forget to control your every single thought!

It is literally impossible!

Your external reality (the one you are experiencing at the moment) is just the result of a small part of conscious thoughts, everything else is continually created by your subconscious and unconscious.

You think you want to win the lottery, you struggle choosing the best numbers, maybe after hours or days of obsessive research, but nothing happens, draw after draw.

And what happens within you?

The belief that you are not meant to win takes root even deeper... and it will be so.

You already know that deep down, in the most hidden part of your Soul, there are different negative thoughts on money, as well as the fear (yes) of not deserving abundance, happiness, and not being able to manage a great wealth.

"So, what needs to be practically done for manifesting a lottery win?"

The answer came, as always, from my Spiritual Guide.

G.A, "Reality is not influenced by your conscious thought, but by *unconscious* deep beliefs, which have been piled up over the decades.

The exercises that I have recommended over time to reschedule your whole being are already valid for manifesting a lottery win.

However, I noticed that you are comfortable with Positive Statements, which are certainly efficient, but you need to know what and how to say them.

Since the most remote ages, the power to create the whole known Universe has been expressed through the Word.

Men and women who master the Word have the power to create the material reality they want.

The Word is alive, resonates, and creates.

If you don't understand this concept, you are still far from commanding your power."

Following my Angelic Guide's directions, after a detailed work on the Words' power, I have drawn up for you some Positive Statements which, if used correctly, will work incessantly to create the wealth and victory reality you aim for.

To ensure that they work, these powerful statements must be read in absolute awareness, focusing above all on the words highlighted in bold that will lead the way for manifesting the winning of money.

You need to perceive, word by word, the vibration caused by each statement all over your body, your mind, and your soul; this is proof that it is working.

Immediately after each statement, visualizing yourself winning the lottery and receiving money will be second nature; this is the right time to thank by making your whole Being vibrate to the sound of every single "Thank you."

You are now ready to begin the transformation journey that will make you powerful and capable of creating wealth and abundance in your existence.

When to Use These Powerful Statements?

There is no limit, as long as it is done in whole participation and a high concentration.

They shall be repeated out loud, at least audible to you, because of the vibrational power; if you also want to repeat them mentally during the day (when you are with other people, at work, or in public), this will help you to focus and go in a state of acceptance of wealth and predisposition to win.

After a while, if the work is done with burning Heart and Will, you will begin to see around you the first manifestations of wealth and money; the fear of poverty will no longer be your traveling companion.

Powerful Statements to Win the Lottery

- **I deserve** to win the lottery. **Thank you, thank you, thank you.**
- **I am so happy and grateful** to manifesting **now** a big lottery win. **Thank you, thank you, thank you.**
- **My destiny** is to win thousands of dollars in a lottery. **Thank you, thank you, thank you.**
- **I'm so** grateful to the Universe for letting me **win** the lottery!
- **Winning** the jackpot is something I do naturally. **Thank you, thank you, thank you.**
- **Choosing the winning numbers** comes easily to me. **Thank you, thank you, thank you.**
- **My mind and heart are** focused and connected with the universal power of luck. **Thank you, thank you, thank you.**
- **I am** naturally lucky to win the lottery. **Thank you, thank you, thank you.**
- **I am** deeply bound to the universal power of luck. **Thank you, thank you, thank you.**
- My family and friends **benefit greatly** from my lottery profits. **Thank you, thank you, thank you.**
- **I am firmly convinced** that I can win the lottery. **Thank you, thank you, thank you.**
- **My faith** in a big lottery win is getting stronger. **Thank you, thank you, thank you.**
- **I can** win plenty of money in a lottery **with my creative power. Thank you, thank you, thank you.**

In these Powerful Statements, there is an immense creative ability that only your Intention can turn on.

Do not be surprised by how the universe will decide to shower you with material and spiritual blessings; know that those who care and force themselves to spread Abundance, Wealth, and Beauty in their life and the world, are greatly loved and protected and are *never* left alone.

Now you have efficient tools to set out to conquer the rich and prosperous life you deserve.

Final Remarks

"Coming into the world is not enough. It is to revive that we are born. Everyday."

Pablo Neruda

"Hello? Good morning, I am calling from HR for last week's hiring interview.

I wanted to inform you that you have been chosen to be part of our staff, the salary is very interesting...

Can we make an appointment to define the details...? "

The inescapable process of renewal had begun to bear fruit.

The fear was still there, but I would not pull back anymore. I still had a lot to learn; there were still many questions to ask and answers to get.

This was just the beginning.

G.A, "Now you know; the Law of Attraction makes every human being manifesting what resonates with him because it is born from inside. The growth path is long, but you have the opportunity to live it in prosperity and to limit suffering.

Everything that you manifest is your responsibility, but it all helps to open the heart and expand the consciousness.

You are still afraid of not making it, but be calm and know; I am with you at any time, I never leave you alone, and without my Love.

Do not rush. You have a lot to think about.

And a lot to talk about."

Everything can change now.

Let the journey begin.

The Angel of the Law of Attraction: The Practical Exercises to Develop Your Skills to Quickly Manifest Money, Success and Prosperity.

Preface

"To those who have, it will be given,

and he will be in wealth;

and to those who do not have, even what he has will be taken away"

Jesus – from the Gospel according to Matthew

In conversation with my Angelic Guide, this Jesus' expression came out often, and it always seemed to be a paradox that whoever has receives even more, and whoever has nothing, is deprived even of that little.

Indeed, it is difficult to understand the words of the Master if you are not prepared to accept a broader vision of how the reality we live in works.

I had the opportunity to read several books on the Law of Attraction or Law of Resonance but, to be fair, there was always something that did not figure out completely.

I felt like I was dealing with *spiritual marketing* when it came to practicality.

In fact, everything proposed to turn on the Law of Attraction did not work with me or worked partially, and only for a certain period of time.

The suggested practice was not wrong in itself, but there was more to understand, a real knowledge of how things really stand inside us, how they move, and what they produce.

Yes, everything is moving inside and, consequently, outside of us.

So I concluded that the discontinuity in the functioning of the Law of Attraction, despite all the proposed techniques, was due to a lack of fluidity and awareness.

This practical handbook was created to solve this need; it is deliberately short and easy to understand because too many words can cause only confusion.

Hundreds of texts on the Law of Attraction, more or less authoritative, are on the market, so those wishing to explore more have nothing to worry about in this regard.

There is something for everyone.

The techniques explained in this writing were recommended to me by my Angelic Guide; together, we tried to make them easily applicable every day, increase each individual's quality of life, and improve their material well-being.

The draft of the text turned out to be complicated in some moments because we ardently wanted the time spent reading and putting into practice the reprogramming techniques to produce not only tangible results but also profound self-satisfaction, which is the basis of the aware activation of the Law of Resonance.

Having followed the same path I propose in this handbook and being deeply convinced of the concrete results that can be achieved, I could actively work on perfecting the techniques described here to —speed up— without sacrificing the quality of the experience itself, the achievement goals.

I used em dashes with the word speed up because, as you already know, hurry is the enemy of concentration and keeps you from guiding your life.

The previous booklet **The Law of Attraction Explained by the Angels. How to attract money and prosperity. A Voice from Quiet Vol. 1** is an emotional-mental preparation for these practical exercises.

These two handbooks were intentionally not put into a single volume together, because theory and practice must follow a precise order otherwise, the experience loses its impact and does not settle in our Being.

All of this is necessary to drive change.

At this point, I just have to wish you (and me) good work.

Chapter 1: Shaping, Cleaning, and Marking

"If you keep doing what you have always done, you will keep getting what you have always had."
Warren G. Bennis

How is it possible that certain things can be achieved without effort while others seem insurmountable?

How is it possible that some people who already know The Law of Attraction can obtain minimal results and others who have never looked at the issue have a full and rich existence from many points of view?

Why are the changes in my life not the ones that I want?

These and other similar questions were continually addressed to my Guardian Angel in our conversations.

We talked about it for a long time because it took a while before the new truth definitively took the place of the old and limiting beliefs.

I clearly could not control my thoughts one by one about the concept of money and wealth on which all my earthly experiences were based. It would have been a difficult and useless work; there was too much to *clean* in both my conscious and subconscious mind... (Not to mention my unconscious).

However, as my Angelic Guide explained to me, everything existing in me was not to be destroyed but transmuted through the Shaping, Cleaning, and Marking work.

This is a daily task because it is the basis of all the techniques we will deal with later.

In my previous booklet (the 6 Steps of Power), it was explained what to do to use the Law of Resonance consciously; that is the development, with constant practice, of some qualities including Faith, Gratitude, and Forgiveness.

Guardian Angel, "It may seem unlikely, but even those who believe they have a lot of Faith, Gratitude, and true Forgiveness ability, have a lot of practice ahead of them if they really want to settle these qualities.

People are often invited to provoke new beliefs, through new thoughts, about money or wealth, with the result of engulfing their minds even more.

Old and new begin an unrelenting fight.

Indeed, it would be nice if the old beliefs could be easily eradicated by replacing them with new ones.

It is not so!

And even if you succeeded after a long time through a draining demolition work, you would still have to wait much longer for the new thought to be deep-seated, with the same tenacity as the old."

ME, "So whoever has limiting concepts about money or wealth, in general, is condemned to live in poverty and limitation?"

G.A, "I did not say that. I just showed you what is said about mental re-conditioning. I say that when things drag on, you get tired and quit the work. You already have plenty of mental and emotional material to work on; do it!

Here I offer a different path to choose.

The work is always challenging, but the results are encouraging along the way."

ME, "It is not easy to understand. Can you give me a practical example?"

G.A, "Sure. Take a common thought or belief about the wealth of those who often live in financial difficulties, such as 'I do not and will never have enough money to live in dignity and fulfill my wishes'"

ME, "Okay (I knew what he was talking about, this thought was fixed in my mind)."

G.A, "Consciously or unconsciously, this expression has been repeated every day for years, by the media too. Even out loud. This is a hard belief to eradicate.

But we can proceed differently; that is, we will use the strength of this belief through Shaping, Cleaning, and Marking."

ME, "How?"

G.A, "Stay here at this very moment with this thought and watch it actively and carefully without judging. Watch each word with awareness as the sentence forms in your mind and feel the emotions that arise from it.

Do not judge."

It hurt a lot; it burned in the chest. It was a dragon spitting fire on me, and I thought I was about to explode.

But then something happened.

The pain began to lower, more and more.

Conscious attention and lack of judgment extinguished the suffering, and a magnificent sense of peace followed.

I was, simply, not afraid anymore.

G.A, "You can now start shaping this thought reformulating it correctly, cleaning it from the dirt and dross left by the Fire, and marking it with the same Fire in your Heart 'I always have money in abundance to live my life joyfully and serenely and fulfill my wishes. Thanks.'"

This applies to all the wrong and limiting beliefs that prevent you from having money and living a prosperous and satisfying life."

I knew I had a lot of these kinds of thoughts, but I realized that at the core of them, there was the fear of poverty; I decided that this would have been the main work.

G.A, "Check the most frequent worries and feelings of discomfort; these are the thoughts to work on right away. Bring attention to them because when there is restlessness, there is a lack of forgiveness. Apply the Shaping, model what you would like to think; proceed with the Cleaning, removing those parts of thought where the dirt concentrates, *visually* cleaning with soap and water; complete with the Marking, re-forming from the old, the new thought. This will immediately begin to produce feelings of well-being.

Use your breath, your friend, at a regular rhythm, and with each inhalation and exhalation, brand the regenerated thought in your consciousness.

At first, you will struggle to concentrate, it will seem that nothing concrete happens, but with time and constancy, you will see the results manifested in your reality.

There is no need to work convulsively on every thought; the important thing is to operate on the recurring ones, which are responsible for your negative state of mind.

This is enough to trigger the change."

The decision was made instantly; I would have applied Shaping, Cleaning, and Marking to every thought, action, and aspect of my life. Whenever something caused me discomfort, I proceeded with these techniques to not have limitations of any kind on my path.

I constantly strive to bring attention and undiscerning observation to every thought that rejects prosperity and abundance in my life.

I take note of what it is.

I always do it, better and better.

I began to breathe like I did not for a long time.

Chapter 2: The 5 Physical/ Mental Rescheduling Techniques of Alignment with the Intentions of Soul Prosperity

"Father, if you want, take this cup away from me!

However, your will be done, not mine."

Jesus

From the Gospel, according to Luke

G.A, "The Law of Resonance does not crash with your soul's mission in this life. However, it is necessary to understand that no one, in heaven and on earth, has decided that you accomplish what you were born for in poverty, solitude, and sadness.

Unless you choose it yourself.

Wealth and satisfaction have been provided for all, and you are here to solve the problem of economic subsistence once and for all.

The aim is to observe without judging the fears and doubts of the mind, to let the soul and the higher forces intervene.

Always ask yourself what job you like the most and how it can become a blessing not only for you but also for the world; the same world that needs you to be satisfied and successful people.

G.A, "In the society of the future, men will have already acquired certain soul abilities, and wealth and material abundance will be part of their reality, as deadlines and debts are part of yours.

The men of today who have definitively solved the problem of economic subsistence do not have a dose of fear in their minds of running out of money or feel guilty for having it. They know exactly that money cannot be owned but loved, like any other form of energy that, properly used, improves existence. They are absolutely aware that the amount of economic well-being is directly proportional to the love for their life mission.

In the future, money will be considered a spiritual tool and used to understand one's personal and profound relationship with the feeling of *lack* and guilt. There will never be a desire to accumulate wealth for a non-existent sense of safety, but to carry out extraordinary life missions soaked with love and sacred light."

My Angelic Guide told me this truth in a long moment of despair. My crises were never trivial and fleeting, but they always dug deep, and I needed to know how things really stood to emerge from the abyss. I was looking for Hope and Faith. I earnestly hoped that my suffering was not vain and that sooner or later, it would bring me in the right direction.

The awareness of who and whose children we are, the Heart opening, and the constant observation of myself, inside and out, represented the turning point of my existence and instilled that fullness of life that I never dared to hope.

I know that there is a long way to go and that it will not end in this existence, but I also know that everything I conquered will never be taken away from me, neither with physical death.

Finally, remember that any change must take root deeply by constantly listening to your soul, or you are likely to fall back into old habits, and you will have no choice but resentment and disappointment.

The time factor is very subjective, but as my Guide always suggests, do not hurry; on the contrary, feeling to live in an eternal present helps to *perceive* what we want into our existence as already achieved.

However, if you really do not succeed and the anxiety for the final result bugs you, face everything, do not suffer it, and accept it until this feeling extinguishes by itself. From these ashes, peace will arise.

Do it whenever you feel it necessary. Even today, I face everyday uncertainties in this way, and I can tell you that they no longer dominate me as they once did.

I am finally (most of the time) my own mistress.

This is my wish for all of you too.

Chapter 3: The Virtual Tattoo

"Getting a tattoo is a journey, not a destination."

Vince Hemingson

I will not dwell on personal considerations about the rescheduling techniques I introduced in the previous chapter.

I will leave the word to my beloved Angelic Guide.

I will let her speak directly to you, as she did with me when everything was still confusing, and I was just beginning to see the light at the end of the tunnel.

I am sure that the benefits I have obtained and that still today (with amazement and satisfaction) I get are intended not only for me but for those who, like me, were afraid every day of not making it.

G.A, "This technique has very ancient origins, and since then, people have used it when they want to imprint in themselves (or bring to conscious awareness every day) a characteristic or quality.

Even today, in Western countries, the tattoo is used not only for pleasure but to *remember* and create the best version of one's being, through drawings and writings, created, according to your feelings.

It is not necessary, however, to actually fill your body with them to bring wealth and money into your life.

This ancient custom can be used in a *virtual* way, that is, by a visualization work.

You can proceed like this; create a mental image that represents your idea of wealth (you can also draw it or search on the internet and choose the one that inspires you the most). It can be a six-zero bank check, a wallet full of banknotes, a cascade of golden coins, or you can use the classic symbols of wealth; a full cornucopia, a pomegranate, a bunch of grapes.

Once you have chosen the image, it must bring you a very strong feeling of well-being and satisfaction, if not, change the symbol.

Now give this feeling a color, and put your personal image of wealth in this color; after that, get the *virtual* tattoo in a part of your body that you like, and every time you want to introduce more money in your life, place your left hand on this tattoo while you visualize it, and say THANK YOU three times.

This procedure strengthens the energy of attraction and gratitude in you."

Chapter 4: Satisfaction of Your Life

"He who is not contented with what he has, would not be contented with what he would like to have."

Socrates

G.A, "I have already explained, previously, that feeling good and grateful is already in itself a part of the work of bringing wealth into your life.

However, Satisfaction is another thing; it is the trigger mechanism of the Law of Attraction.

Satisfaction comes with the feeling of being in the right place at the right time; it is seeing the glass full (not half full like the optimist).

It is that feeling of wealth within yourself that still claims abundance as a full right in a kind of virtuous circle.

The more you have, the more you want, without being touched by greed, by the feeling of lack, but as a natural condition of your being.

Satisfaction is the feeling that your life (according to the highest and deepest vision that only you know) is perfect and worth living; carrying out the Mission of your soul is glorifying the Creator with your life."

ME, "But how and where can I find satisfaction if I am going through a bad and heavy moment economically speaking? I don't want to mourn or play the victim, I know there are other aspects of my life that I like, and I am thankful for that. But money is never enough, as hard as I try, I can't find satisfaction in this sense."

G.A, "It is absolutely true that pretending to live in a reality different from the actual one leads nowhere, let alone satisfied. I would never suggest such a thing!

Satisfaction, as I understand it, can never arise from a need of the mind or body that has not been reflected in reality yet. That is called illusion or fantasy.

When I say "True Satisfaction" I mean that inner state that goes beyond the momentary lack of something specific, and that goes towards a higher meaning of your life. It is dedicating to carrying out a lofty task that brings you closer to your true divine nature. Only like this, it is possible to perceive the usefulness and importance of your existence."

ME, "So, dissatisfaction arises from an illusion or a wrong feeling of how things really stand."

G.A, "Yes and, more specifically, from the fear that your life has no meaning if things do not develop as you want, or if you do not have what you want; and this causes the uselessness, unworthiness feeling.

Therefore, turning your gaze towards a wider and higher horizon radically changes the meaning of everything, you regain possession of the higher purpose of life. The dissatisfaction feeling for what you considered necessary for your happiness becomes secondary or even marginal.

But that's not all; it is right now, with this feeling that, like on a wonderful Christmas morning, everything you had wished for in the past will be given to you by the Universe when you least expect it.

Money and wealth begin to flow into your existence like never before, bringing even more satisfaction to the beauty of your life."

ME, "Letting go of something I crave is so difficult..."

G.A, "You misunderstood me. You often concentrate on the natural pursuit of joy and satisfaction that humans carry out in their existence, in small areas, or in having objects and successful works. And this is not wrong in itself, everyone chooses his way according to certain inner beliefs. What slows down and creates frustration and disappointment is the little attention towards you and all your time spent changing external reality.

So you will get nothing.

When you look in the mirror and want to comb your hair, do you act on yourself or your reflection?

The answer is obvious!

Similarly, craving for something and not being able to get it means that you are combing the reflection, wasting creative energy directing it exclusively outside of you.

Go back to serenity within you, rejoin your divine nature, and widen the horizon. What you call letting go, I call it an act of faith and love."

Chapter 5: Light Charity

"I had forgotten how much light there is in the world,

till you gave it back to me."

Ursula K. Le Guin

Material charity is not replaced by Light charity.

My aim here is to lead a greater number of people to live in abundance by ensuring that those who are not rich yet can benefit from help to speed up their evolutionary process, up to a joyful life.

Those who are already in tune with their soul's purpose and see wealth flowing in large quantities are called to increase anything they can and to promote the evolutionary development of the human species.

If you believe it is right to give to charity to people begging on the street, do it!

But remember that there is a lot to protect and support; from art to holistic sciences, to the expansion and diffusion of libraries even in small towns, volunteer groups in hospitals (supporting both those who undergo heavy cures and their families), and groups that generally protect the weaker categories, such as children and the elderly.

Last but not least, associations you know and trust that spend the assumed money constructively.

Try to remain anonymous for the Light Charity as much as possible; in doing so, the wealth started from you will return to you to a larger extent.

G.A, "The word Charity must make it clear that in addition to material aids to those who still cannot attend to their needs, there must be a specific intention in wanting to bring *well-being* inwardly to people in need.

No one can or must overstep the free will of another, in any way, justifying himself for having done so for *his* sake; every human being has the right, if he chooses so, to experience his own "Hell on Earth" until he has enough and is ready for change."

ME, "So what is my and everyone's role, seen in this light?"

G.A, "Your role, in addition to concrete help, is to bring your presence and awareness where there are lack, poverty, and misery; be a sort of -- example-- of how different life can be if lived with joy and satisfaction.

When you look towards need, do not let sadness dominate you, but know that, since you are there, everything can be all right, and that where there is a situation of pain, this is immediately transmuted into a situation of peace and serenity.

Always aim for transmutation rather than simple transformation because the first one provides for a higher spiritual elevation and, therefore, eternal.

Whatever experience you live, firsthand or through others, try not to lose your center; keep your joy, or serenity, to bring positivity even outside of you, without preventing the development of what is.

By doing so, you will not block the Charity of Light that starts and returns to you continuously, creating a virtuous circle and a constant blessing for all those who have to do with you.

Any negative feeling or thought that will try to touch you will pass through, without leaving negative traces; on the contrary, you will have stoically endured the temptation to get involved in external pain.

After all, if there were no temptations, you would never have the measure of your strength."

Chapter 6: Allowing and Receiving: Opening the Golden Door

"To come into the world is receiving a whole universe as a gift."

Jostein Gaarder

All of us have the right and duty, every day, to improve our economic situation and, certainly, do not believe that money is an obstacle to our evolution as an individual.

Unfortunately, this is not always the case; most of the time, we think (because our education requires it) that money and prosperity are not an expression of the divine, of the Creator's love for His creatures.

In fact, I learned the hard way that money does not change a man, neither improves him nor makes him worse, but it only reveals his nature.

The Law of Attraction acts at a deeper level.

It is the unconscious that is the soul that creates most of the reality surrounding us.

The mind tries to change something in its life; however, only the soul knows that the change, to manifest itself in reality, must be profound and sometimes painful.

The perception of abundance and love needs to change; external conditions will change but only as an inevitable consequence of an internal change.

This premise was necessary to introduce the technique proposed by my Angelic Guide in the best way.

Realizing that religious, fake moral conditioning, and old education pose a threat to our true fulfillment is fundamental for a clean work of wealth creation.

It is not our fault!

But it is our responsibility to start change so that we can allow and receive the abundance of everything and the wealth we deserve.

When my Guardian Angel told me about the Golden Door technique, my first reaction was to make it known as soon as possible; it was unthinkable that this truth was just mine.

G.A, "Through the Law of Attraction, we receive what we give because it is part of our real essence.

To have a resonance, selfless acts must be full of vibrations of a specific quality and not as often happens, motivated by ethics and empty morals; (I do this because it is right but my feeling and my heart are addressed to something else).

And usually, this feeling comes from a vision of lack and poverty and not of well-being; altruism, if not felt, becomes basically pity!

The Golden Door technique that allows you to receive wealth is possible only when you have achieved a certain awareness and clarity about your goals and a certain self-observation; when you are aware that there is no need for judgment outside and inside you.

Begin now to have clarity and to know that chance (and chaos) does not really exist, so you have decided to take full responsibility for your reality.

The Golden Door is a thin center placed on the heart chakra; its opening allows the entrance and constant flow of wealth into your life.

Mind you, I said *flow*, not collect.

The moment you block the flow, the Golden Door will close and will no longer allow the entrance of those energies conducive to wealth

So behave like this; after a series of breaths that promote relaxation and inner peace, visualize a closed golden door at the height of your heart.

Define it in detail as you like, as long as it transmits you the feeling of wealth. Now think about a golden stream made of gold coins and open the door. This stream flows in you with every breath and envelops your every thought and emotion, and thus charged, it returns to the Universe, which will send it to every human being on Earth.

From this moment, through the Golden Gate, you have the power to allow entrance and receive wealth, constantly sharing it with the rest of humanity.

Always monitor the flow of wealth during your day so that you are aware all the time of the flow of abundance outside and inside you; this especially in the early days until the practice has become a good habit and every atom of your body is aligned with the flow.

You can also direct the power of the flow to something specific; a sizeable salary increase, extra income, or an important gift you desire.

And again, you can use this technique to increase the feeling of selflessness and generosity; always be honest and do not judge yourself if you are unwilling to bring financial help to others. Everything is learned and developed as a quality, and constant effort is always rewarded.

Remember; do not rush but love and dedicate to work."

Chapter 7: Acceptance and Gratitude

"Lord, grant me the strength to change the things I can, the serenity to deal with the things I cannot change, and the wisdom to know the difference."

Saint Francis

When my Guardian Angel told me about the latest technique, I objected by saying that the topic had been covered many times, and I did not believe it was necessary to deepen.

As usual, I was wrong.

What is taken for granted is what is worth lingering on again and again.

So to close the work session, the seal consists of this last step; acceptance and gratitude.

G.A, "Whenever you work with Shaping, Cleaning and Marking on your thoughts and emotions, continue with the life satisfaction technique and do Light Charity, and, finally, Allow and Receive through the Golden Door opening, end with these words, as one of the greatest Masters of all time taught us; 'Father, Thy will be always done, not mine. Thank you with all my heart.'

This impetus of love prepares you for receiving what is best for you in quantity and quality; what the Universe has in store for you is always compatible with your life mission and is always benevolent.

Accepting the reality of your existence does not stop the flow of wealth and prosperity towards you, on the contrary, it makes you fully responsible for your life, and it gives you the power to place yourself on another vibratory plane; **the wealth one.**

You cannot choose the Light if you do not know the darkness, and in the same way, only by observing the current situation and accepting it fully, you prepare yourself for change.

Nothing and no one can take away from you what is yours by birthright, so do not be afraid, do not rush, and enjoy the journey.

Even if you were born several times on this planet, your current life is still one of a kind.

You have come to this point because you have worked hard on yourself, incarnation after incarnation, and today you finally have the chance to consciously and forever bring well-being and wealth into your existence and this world so that everyone can benefit from it.

Be proud of your unique and magnificent, although painful, work.

This is also why you are much loved."

Final Remarks

"Begin to be now what you will be hereafter."
William James

At the end of the writing of these two handbooks, I lingered in conversation with my Guardian Angel, displaying doubts and perplexities; in fact, I was not sure that everything I had acknowledged in this long journey, made not only of theory but also practice, had been adequately presented.

We chose the direct way to talk about money and wealth without getting lost in too many conversations and mental ramblings, leading by the hand those who wanted to venture into this experience, in the belief that if even a tenth part of the truth breached the heart and mind of the reader, his life would never be the same; he would have had the answers to his many questions.

So, as always, with a grateful and confident heart, I decided to live this experience increasing the satisfaction of my life.

I will conclude with one of the last recommendations of my Angel, in the hope that it can be an inspiration for you as it always is for me.

For everything else that is and what will be, I can only say; thank you so much.

G.A, "The more you give, the more you get; this is the secret to success.

Consider yourself a hero in giving to others Love and Happiness, Wealth, and Creativity, and you will have contributed to bringing Abundance at every level in this world.

Handle, kindly but firmly, your fear of running out of money, job, family, but share the new worldview and make it manifest.

Never settle, be every day satisfied with your life.

May you be blessed."

The Angel of the Law of Attraction: The Secret to Happy Relationships by Developing Your Abilities to Receive Friendship, Kindness and Love

Preface

"Happiness is love, nothing else.
A man who is capable of love is happy."
Hermann Hesse

Love, love, always love.

What would any man or woman be without Love?

I do not claim to know the evolutionary path of every human being, but whatever it is, without Love, everything is empty and lifeless.

You can achieve important personal goals, but if you do not have true Love beside you, everything fades, turns gray, even the greatest enthusiasm.

This topic was extensively discussed with my Guardian Angel, and, despite my skepticism, I fully understood that what He meant by true Love had a different *warmth* from the concept that we develop in the course of our life about Love.

We are creators of our own lives, and the same goes for the man or woman of our dreams.

Unfortunately for us, even if we do not realize it, we constantly change our minds about what we really want and, therefore, we change our choices too.

Actually, we should think that every time anything we have ardently wanted and worked for materializes in our life, we perform a magical act; that is to say, we have deliberately mastered the Law of Attraction for our benefit. We have been able to maintain over time an intention through thoughts and actions without losing its energy, and this intention has manifested itself concretely because we have allowed it to flow through us, without inappropriate changes of direction, doubts, or fears.

The delays, hardships, setbacks, and the various difficulties on our path that divide us from what we want, depend only and exclusively on us; we have the necessary help to stay on course, but only we can do the work; free will is never questioned and nobody can meddle with our *freedom* of choice.

Free will is an extraordinary gift, but also terrible because every second reminds us that the reality we live in is all our responsibility, for better or for worse.

Wanting True Love in our life is not enough to make it manifest out of the blue; maybe before arriving, there will be little loves, preparatory for the Great Love, stories that need to end in this existence because they started in a previous life, but all remarkable for our spiritual growth.

The goal is to see perfection in everything, even in delays and setbacks; you are getting ready for the best.

However, it is good to remember that whatever action you take to find true love, you are interacting with the will of other human beings, so the choice must be made on both sides. Never impose yourself if there is no emotional correspondence.

Speaking of creation through the Law of Attraction to find true Love, it is not enough to program ourselves mentally. The rules explained in my previous handbooks also apply here; be satisfied with yourself, know that the best for you already exists, and above all, be alert; to be --here and now-- at the moment activates the ability to create your reality.

I had the opportunity to speak with single women and men of different ages, and all of them (albeit to varying degrees) dream of a sentimental fulfillment. Instead, I noticed that those who do not want to be emotionally too involved in sentimental stories have often and willingly loved and lost.

Or they are convinced like this.

Actually, when you love deeply, you never lose, perhaps you suffer and feel alone, but if you have eyes to see and an open heart, the truth appears different.

I met who, not knowing how to find his sweetheart anymore, turned even to fortune tellers, gurus, and stuff like that, wasting time and money.

In short, at some point, love becomes a dysfunctional thought, a pain rather than a source of joy and happiness.

And I know from my own experience.

Since I was a child, I did not care about dolls, I did not have a strong maternal instinct, even if I loved children, and I really liked spending time with them (even today), but I continually imagined my charming prince in any romantic situation.

My adolescence and first flirtations passed, and at about twenty-three, I did not meet my true love yet.

Today after many years, I realize that at that age, I shouldn't have worried so much, but it was devastating for me; everyone, friends and relatives, were engaged, married, or about to get married; who was single was under sixteen.

And here began the serious research.

Chapter 1: Remembering Myself

"Be worthy love, and love will come."

Louisa May Alcott

At the time, I did not have a close dialogue with my Guardian Angel but only profound reflections with myself that, I would later know, were inspired by my Angelic Guide.

Before meeting True Love, my current husband, I went through some very dark months, during which I seriously thought about giving up love. I did not want to waste time and suffer anymore.

But meanwhile, I was suffering!

I did not know the Law of Attraction if not marginally, I did not have the opportunity to analyze the subject with my Angel, but what happened in those months was just the demonstration of how it acts, whether we realize it or not, in every aspect of our life.

And the field of relationships is no exception.

As I said before, analyzing the topic of Love and the Law of Attraction with my Guardian Angel, I also examined my own experience (similar to that of many other men and women), to fully understand what really happened to me in that period, on a deep level, to produce the change in my love life, overnight.

ME, "You know, many people ask me how to have a fulfilling and profound love story; why, despite their continuous attempts to find True Love, do they have only conflicting stories that always end badly. I try to answer these questions, but the topic is complex, and I'm afraid of harming more than actually helping. I am uncomfortable."

Guardian Angel, "You are in trouble because you do not know how things really work, even if you experienced something that led you to your life partner."

ME, "In spite of myself?"

G.A, "Despite your ignorance about how things work on an energetic level and the Law of Attraction. Everything is subjected to this Law because everything is synchronous, nothing happens or does not happen by chance. There are some things to keep in mind if you want to take this path consciously, otherwise, times may get very long. You can also risk not running into True Love in this life, or not recognizing it, switching from a story to another until you wear out, or throw in the towel.

What you experienced, that led you on the same path of your True Love, you have built it day by day with pain and, finding the answers, more or less consciously, succeeding in vibrating in such a way that you met he who is your husband today."

ME, "But can we try to recreate in steps what I experienced to make it useful for others, perhaps without all that suffering?"

G.A, "You can do everything, but not avoiding suffering! Not because there is someone in the highest heaven who enjoys seeing the men and women suffer, but simply because any change requires effort, and this causes a certain amount of pain.

But it can be contained and lived with awareness, to limit its duration.

Women give birth with pain, but this does not mean that there are no suitable aids to reduce suffering."

ME, "The starting question is very common; why do some people find true love right away and others don't, or do they find it after a long time? What is the difference between them?"

G.A, "The difference is substantial! But don't believe that those who, in this life, immediately find the ideal life partner have been lucky or privileged. They certainly worked hard in their past lives, with effort and pain, up to they reaped the benefits of their strain before others.

And to enjoy them.

However, it is good to remember that the work to keep a loving relationship alive never ends, and it changes from time to time, just like life experiences do."

ME, "What can we do then, to speed up the process? Nobody wants to wait to be 80 for their soulmate!"

G.A, "You are obsessed with haste! But I understand, you live in the illusion of time, and you have to deal with it."

ME, "In fact, I know it well."

I was going to indirectly recall my personal magic of when I came across my Love, but this time I had a guiding light on my forehead to shed light on all those creative energies that turned on.

I used the Law of Attraction as a powerful magical act to materialize what I had helped to create; love with a capital L.

Chapter 2: Shed Light in Yourself

"To love oneself is the beginning
of a lifelong romance."
Oscar Wilde

G.A, "Let's start with an important point; self-appreciation.

It seems an obvious concept, everyone thinks they appreciate themselves. But it is not so. Everyone wants the best for themselves but often, what really happens is to compromise immediately to keep from being alone. Risking is essential if you want to achieve the best result.

Do you really accept yourself for who you are?

Do you love yourselves?

If you do not do it first, no one will.

Try to stand in front of a mirror, with simple clothes or almost naked, and see how you feel.

The arising emotions are the same ones felt for you by the others. So if you love, accept, and esteem yourself, others will respond to you with the same vibrational frequency.

Likewise, you attract True Love to you.

External reality as a result of the Law of Attraction perfectly returns your feeling.

This exercise is useful whenever you want to control and subsequently strengthen self-esteem and love.

It will also help you to appreciate every other aspect of your life, considering everything as a beautiful gift in your reality and increasing the love and passion for everything you do.

So, stop judging yourselves because as you judge yourself, so does the world."

ME, "In the end, we must start from ourselves and never from something that is outside; if the vibratory frequency of who we are looking for is similar to ours, then it manifests itself concretely in reality. This is always due to the Law of Attraction."

G.A, "It's all in resonance. And the world is your mirror. You cannot attract someone to you if he does not have the same vibrations. Even in the stormiest relationships, the other brings to light the deepest characteristics of your psychology so that these are identified and transmuted.

This is the real work that needs to be done in the couple.

Many people often complain about ups and downs in their relationship, even though they love each other very much.

The point is; realize that you have all the tools to make things work, but you must always start from Love, that is, the absence of judgment and complete acceptance of yourself and the other. This step is essential to understand even before meeting the right person; you will have got ahead of the work."

ME, "The start of everything is to love ourselves deeply?"

G.A, "There is no other way; if you want love, you must be *love*, or you will not give love.

The first reason why people look for a satisfying relationship is that they believe they would be happier; living together is not the key to emotional serenity and, most of the time, couples break out because reality does not correspond to their ideal of love.

Daily problems, at some point, are perceived as insurmountable, and one comes to think that the partner is wrong so, we start over with the search for a new romantic relationship, without accepting that if the inner problems are not solved, they will carry them in the next love story.

But even this one will have the same fate as the previous one in different times and ways."

ME, "So what is wrong with us that always pushes us towards suffering?

Are the education received and our childhood traumas also responsible for so much unhappiness?"

G.A, "Partially.

If during your childhood you felt abandoned, mistreated, not listened to, humiliated, and even betrayed, with adulthood, these feelings will be thrown out for a match with a partner who will resound with them. His presence alone is enough to pull these traumas out of you, and if the wounds are not healed, the vicious circle of relationship to relationship will never end.

At first, during the first stages of falling in love, everything seems to be going in joy and happiness, and you feel like you have the love story you dreamed of, the ones you read in fairy tales. But over time, the unchanged wounds will claim their healing, and you cannot ignore them anymore.

However, you have to accept that suffering is not caused by someone you hang out with but by a thin vibration of your interiority that remains there until you decide to observe it to start the transmutation and proceed with the final healing.

Similarly, if you are looking for happiness, you need to accept to look and find it inside yourself; it does not depend on your potential partner.

The power is in your own hands. Besides, as you may have already understood, if you look for the source of your joy in your partner, you will never find it because you will have attracted to you a person who tends to be in disharmony.

Does this sound familiar to you?"

It did!

It had been my basic model before I met my True Love; I always referred to being in a couple, in a future moment, being happy and in love, when all I had to do was be grateful and satisfied with the love in and around me, represented by many people, and to increase it in every moment.

For this reason, at some point, I felt down in the dumps, I hit the depth of the sorrow, and then I started the climb.

At the time, I didn't really know what was happening, despite everything was in transformation.

If I had had more awareness and more spiritual presence, I would have mastered my fear and suffering better.

ME, "However, in the light of what you have explained to me, facing all these demons seems like a long way..."

Chapter 3: Unconditional Love and Possession

"Love does not consist of gazing at each other,

but in looking outward together

in the same direction."

Antoine de Saint-Exupery

G.A, "If you set aside the selfish instincts, the way to go is considerably shortened. The choice to make is to accept with ardent love the people you meet on your path and see their absolute beauty.

I know that it may be difficult if these people bring you suffering and disappointment.

But the attention must be shifted from them to your feelings to identify the root of this discomfort, bring it to light and heal yourself and your current or future relationship."

ME, "And then, can we expect True Love and the love relationship we always wanted?"

G.A, "If you do not focus on the time but the path, it turns out to be more beneficial.

When you are advised to focus your thoughts to achieve a certain goal, you do not want to urge an obsession on a person.

Stop thinking of your current or eventual partner as something to own; possession is the opposite of the spiritual evolution and a friend of fear.

Fear kills everything good in you, and that would help you get closer to True Love.

Face the fact that no matter how much you want to control your partner (real or presumed), you do not have the power. Possession is not a sign of true love but an insane and unhealthy attachment that sooner or later will lead to humiliation and violence. Passion, if not surrounded by pure love, does not feed your soul but degrades it to the lowest and animal instincts.

Love brings you closer to the Divine, does not make you tremble with fear at the thought of being rejected or left by our loved ones."

ME, "But, this possessive way of seeing love seems to be widespread."

G.A, "It is. Your newscasts are full of crimes of passion, often involving innocents. There is no love there, but only mental confusion; the partner becomes property, and we prefer to destroy him rather than choosing to love him unconditionally and leaving him free to be and do what he wants.

If you can have such a feeling in your heart, you would realize that what you love without conditions is yours and nothing can be stolen from you.

The more you love unconditionally, the more you are surrounded by people who love you; there is no lack or loneliness."

ME, "I understand what you mean. But as usual, it is easier said than done."

G.A, "It depends on how tired you are of living the same situations. The choice is yours. It is also your responsibility for the life you live.

External reality is the mirror of internal reality, and it can only react to how you are and to your changes.

Very often, you push away the meeting with your soulmate because you are victims of your sense of guilt and your undeclared anger; the people you deal with are the most suitable for you to bring to light and observe these situations, resolving them once and for all.

Once you cleaned the field, you will be ready for the big meeting.

However, as I already said before, this does not mean that you do not have to work with your soulmate if you want a true and fulfilling relationship. You always work hard, but with the love of your life, it is certainly more enjoyable."

Chapter 4: Your Soulmate Really Exists: You Are Already Connected and You Do Not Know It

"Love is space and time measured by the heart."

Marcel Proust

At this point, I was quite aware that each of us, thanks to the Law of Attraction, calls the best situations and the most suitable people to our life purpose.

Finding Love and living a whole life with our soulmate can also be part of it if we choose it. Even though the path may be difficult and demanding at times, we must never lose faith.

Our Soul knows what we need, and the Universe also provides help on our path.

We must always remember that to activate the Law of Attraction, our attention and our constant work must be turned inside us, to our deepest feeling, only in this *place* it is possible to carry out those changes that will manifest even in reality.

We are always responsible for better or for worse; there is no one out there to blame; before deciding what to do, it is necessary to choose how to be to start behaving differently and change.

In this regard, I asked my Guide, "Is there the ideal partner for every human being, with whom spend a lifetime? Can you speed up the moment of the meeting?"

G.A, "Surely, by monitoring your moods and shaping some habits, you fortify the energy that attracts you to each other.

Actually, you are already connected, and you do not know it.

It is not necessary to know but essential to feel inside of you.

You already know the power of Gratitude; this force helps you attract your Soulmate too.

Being grateful to feel the love around you will attract great Love more quickly.

Gratitude needs to be strengthened every day for everything in your life, even the ones you take for granted.

A good exercise to be grateful is to write in a notebook, every day, at least ten reasons to thank the Universe, and reread them throughout the day, experiencing joyful emotions.

You will be amazed to discover how much Love there is already in your existence.

In the meantime, carry out your life acting like you have a partner; so, sleep on one side of the bed, make breakfast for two, act and think like in couple, feel the loving and beneficial presence of Love every day next to you.

And, be always thankful for that."

ME, "But our mind knows that there is no one next to us. It will not be easy to fool."

G.A, "It is not about fooling your mind, but of moving to that particular vibrational frequency where the life with your Soulmate already is.

If you intentionally create the deep emotions you want to see in your reality, paying attention and monitoring your moods, it is only a matter of time; the Law of Attraction will give you what you are, that is Love.

Just let it happen.

Let go, do not anguish with doubts and fears, but find your *permanent center of gravity*, as a famous song says, and keep it as constant as possible.

You already decided to live this existence together even before you were born, so you came on this planet together. You will find each other, do not doubt, you would not feel this profound sense of lack in each other."

ME, "But I know that many people are alone their entire lives, and they do not seem happy with it. Why does it happen?"

G.A, "The Miracle of Love is not precluded to any Soul, even if (before coming to the world) it chose to make its journey on Earth alone.

Its authentic and strong bond with True Love remains intact, even without ever meeting.

However, there are profound reasons if this happens, no one can violate a person's free will, not even we Angels are allowed to. We can only help and support you, whatever your choice is.

If a soul decided to be alone in this life, choosing not to share it with True Love, it is because it has a special mission to fulfill, and this will always support it, greatly reducing the sense of loneliness.

However, we can change our minds; no Soul is condemned to live in isolation.

So, if during your existence, thanks to your work of self-awareness and personal growth, you decide you want True Love, you just have to declare it and head in that direction. Nothing and nobody can prevent it."

Chapter 5: Recognizing and Choosing Each Other: The Beginning of the Journey Together

"Love is that condition in which the happiness of another person is essential to your own."

Robert A. Heinlein

ME, "Sometimes it happens that two soulmates, after having searched and found each other, divide themselves. Some come back together, while others do not. Can you tell me why?"

G.A, "The path of a love story, as I said before, can be filled with obstacles that never depend on the partner, but always on personal unhealed wounds.

And when I talk about healing, I always refer to Forgiveness.

Forgiveness is possible with the opening of your Heart, and this can happen only through Love and Compassion. With constant effort, day by day, you can elevate Love in Forgiveness, towards you, others, and every type of life experience.

You will concretely feel the fire of Forgiveness, Love, and Gratitude, right at the level of the solar plexus, and when it has finished burning, it will have transformed the weight of pain, anger, loneliness into the gold of Love and Compassion.

Love and self-love make this journey together possible.

Literally adoring the Life Partner does not mean being a slave to someone, but being always there for the other, seeing the beauty of his

Soul in every minute of our existence.

Or at least, trying every day to do it.

This is what makes love great.

Yet it happens that despite the effort made, two people decide to divide, and they do not always find each other in the future.

I cannot go into each specific case, yet the problem is always the same; lack of Forgiveness and openness of the Heart.

When, on the other hand, after a separation, the couple gets back stronger than before, then the time spent apart helped them to find and shed light on themselves.

Even if only one partner needed this lonely time, this separation was the cure also for the other, which will have strengthened in the wait of his beloved, in Forgiveness, and the continuous vision of Great Love; when we truly love, we never get lost and feel alone."

ME, "So, do we need to keep thinking about the relationship we want, clarifying inside of us with Love and Forgiveness, Faith and Unconditional Gratitude, being determined, even in times of crisis?"

The moment I asked the question, I realized how much we need to work to achieve our goals and live happily.

What brings us happiness is not the materialization of our material or love desires for sure, but the choice of being satisfied with our life on this Earth.

This results in the full material realization of our most beautiful dreams.

Feeling worthy of the best in the world and being loved is the starting point for the work to be done in every existence, without any judgment towards us or others, nor towards our past or present.

Through the full acceptance with Love, we can glean from that stillness that reconnects us with our deepest Self, letting us be taken by the hand and guided towards the wonderful life we can live.

Chapter 6: Think of the Best Version of Yourself and Make It Happen

"Always be a first-rate version of yourself, instead of a second-rate version

Of somebody else."

Judy Garland

G.A, "Being honest with yourself is very hard, but nobody stops you from thinking as big as you can.

If you intend to find and experience Great Love, you must perceive yourself as great Beings deserving of a lot of Love and include in your life all those qualities we talked about; Love, Forgiveness, Faith, and Gratitude.

Think also of others and perceive them as wonderful beings who come with you on this journey of Love and Knowledge.

In addition to your Soulmate, there are other forms of love in your life, such as family, friends, and even your pets.

Never forget about who has always been by your side since the beginning of life, who has played with you and shared joys and sorrows.

Begin immediately to open your Heart towards them, their memory, and bless them, and all the time spent with them.

The people who surround you, even in your daily challenges, are there to bring out the best part of yourself; with them, you can be honest, at ease, and give your best in all circumstances.

You have the wonderful chance to grow also through comparison with others."

ME, "Is it a kind of preparation for the most important love story of our life?"

G.A, "Living waiting for something or someone to be happy leads nowhere.

At this point, you know.

But neither dragging everyday problems pays back.

We need the courage to live the life we want from the start; there is the risk of making mistakes, but we can always count on the unconditional love around us.

The certainty and joy that the awareness of being able to realize your dreams gives you fuels the fire of Love towards yourself, towards others and puts you on the same path as your soulmate.

Was it like that for you too, right?"

ME, "Yes, I remember it perfectly. Love for my life brought me the Love of my life."

G.A, "Accepting and loving each other is possible only if one can see the wonders of creation and commits to becoming concretely satisfied.

The time you have can be used not to fight your fears but to strengthen faith in the accomplishment of your goals through the loving deeds you choose for yourself and others.

Give unconditional Love and Forgive whenever there are pain and suffering in your life and feelings; be responsible for everything you experience and be happy for it; you have the power to change things, and you can do it right away."

ME, "It sounds easy and difficult at the same time. But I know that the main thing is the daily effort to put into practice this new vision of oneself and the world. But some people struggle much more than others to accept that they are the only ones responsible for their happiness, especially in love."

G.A, "Defining the best version of yourself means knowing at least what you do not want to be and taking the improvement path.

Constant effort is necessary to strengthen within oneself the new habits and thoughts that have formed on new feelings. Blaming others will not change anything in your reality for the better, but it will make it worse. These are all excuses of a lazy mind that knows how demanding the work required by the Soul is, but if it knew how many great rewards it would receive for a little daily effort, it would not make a fuss!

But you are the masters, and you decide whether to take the risk of this new journey or not.

If you keep living by the old patterns, you will always have the usual results, and this is pure madness.

However, Life does not remain inactive; if you do not decide to implement the inner change, something will push you, despite yourself in the right direction.

The difference is in the amount of extra pain and suffering you will go through.

In many cases, you are your own worst enemies."

Final Remarks

"To love for the sake of being loved is human, but to love for the sake of loving

is angelic."

Alphonse de Lamartine

Adopting healthy mental habits is as easy as becoming addicted; it is just a matter of choice.

Perceiving oneself as losers in love is looking outside rather than inside oneself and not realizing that as a result of the Law of Attraction, we live the reality we created very scrupulously (even if unconsciously).

To attract Love, we must get rid of all the negative energy accumulated in our souls over the years and be able to look at what bothers us about others as a problem to be solved in us through the magnificent four; Love, Forgiveness, Faith, and Gratitude.

Everyone has the right and the duty to create well-being in and around him so that he can walk the path for True Love, recognize him and spend his whole life with him.

So, every time you are in a negative mental and emotional state, or you are having a hard time, snap out of it and immerse yourself in the total Love that you want for yourself and your soulmate; this will help you heal your deepest wounds that created the situation you are experiencing.

I will leave you with a piece of advice that my Guardian Angel gave me some time ago and that sometimes when I get anxious, he still reminds me.

I wish each of you to experience your unique love story as soon as possible, fully, and happily for the rest of your life and beyond.

G.A, "Concrete help to get rid of defiling feelings and thoughts, which keep your creative energy low, can be given to you by an ancient practice known, handed down and taught for reconciliation, inner forgiveness, conflict resolution, freedom from fears, worries, and everything that prevents or slows down personal and spiritual evolution.

They call it prayer.

Whenever you feel something different from Love or Compassion, something that produces disharmony, entrust with prayer.

By joining your hands at chest height, turn your Heart to the Universal Love of the Creator and ask for courage, faith, strength, and calm.

Continue with the description of what worries you or simply the discomfort you feel.

Be honest with yourself and identify the root of this pain and your responsibility in creating it.

Nobody judges you, so do not do it.

Forgive yourself, be thankful, and let all evil and suffering go away from you, watch it taken away on the wings of the Angels.

And be happy."

The Angel of the Law of Attraction: The Secret to Constantly Manifest Wellness and Health in Your Life

Preface

"It's even pleasant to be sick when you know that there are people who await your recovery as they might await a holiday."

Anton Chekhov

Immediately after I was forty, I discovered I had breast cancer.

Although every year I undergo specific checks, I did not think I would get sick.

But I did.

It was also one of the worst breast cancers, which is why the therapies following surgery were very heavy and invasive to the point where it took many months after the end of the treatment to get back on track.

Healing is an interior journey, personal first of all, made with Love and also nourished by the Love of those who have shared this experience with me.

Above all, my Guardian Angel and my husband managed with their attention and Presence to make this experience bearable and acceptable.

When we have to face a serious illness firsthand, countless things change within us, the shapes and colors of our reality change too, and not always for the better.

Unknown inner demons and fears are unleashed, and we are called to face them.

I cried from fear when I was diagnosed with cancer, but then I realized that my mind was drawing devastating scenarios, supposing a future that it did not make sense to consider.

It was simply in shock!

So as the days went by and I got ready for everything I had to face, such as surgery, chemotherapy, and radiotherapy, I decided to face my fear to understand, with the help of my Angelic Guide, why some human beings are forced to deal with so many pathologies, and others live healthier.

And above all, why do diseases have to exist in the world

Can we live without being constantly threatened by the idea of becoming seriously ill?

Our Soul, I am sure, is always full of energy and happiness, but we rarely experience these feelings.

We are always at the mercy of some physical or emotional suffering.

Or both.

However, a state of inner harmony is what we all want, and if we pay attention, we realize that this is the starting point for a state of good physical health.

On the contrary, when we have fears and resentments, sooner or later, we will feel the effects on our body.

Yet, there are still those who believe that the two are disconnected.

When I think back on the path of my illness, I still feel a little uneasy in remembering everything I experienced inside and outside of me, the anger and the sense of injustice for something that I did not think I deserved but was happening to me anyway.

My sense of judgment was cruel; I was having a hard time getting myself back and recovering my center.

Aids, as I said, never lacked, and I tried to use them all.

Knowing the Law of Attraction for years, I was distressed by the idea that, in some way, I attracted the disease into my life.

Plus, this type of disease!

I wondered why the ideal conditions for this pathology were created inside me and what would I benefit from all this.

The first thing I realized was that some aspects I thought I knew till that moment, concerning the functioning mechanisms of the Law of Attraction, were only in my mind; I had not enclosed them in my Awareness.

The second thing was that the path was long, and I had to be very patient.

For a long time, I would not have gone anywhere.

The surgery was performed a few days before Christmas, and chemotherapy began immediately after the outcome of the histological examination, which, as I said before, ruled the high aggressiveness of this type of cancer.

It was about mid-January, the eve of my first chemo.

It was cold outside, and I was very distressed; I did not want to *poison* my body with this mix of substances that, however, seemed to be necessary to avoid the risk of relapse.

I was deeply sorry about this.

I felt the consoling presence of my Guardian Angel, and in silence, I asked him the most obvious but also the most painful question; why me?

The answer was not long in coming. He was waiting, as always, for me to be ready to understand.

Chapter 1: We Attract Illness Just Like the Other Experiences

"Who waits to be sick to take care of himself is similar to who begins to dig a well while he is tormented by thirst."

Neil King

Guardian Angel, "Every single human being externally manifests what is inside him.

The reality he lives faithfully reflects his inner world, and this is nourished on different levels, the physical, emotional, and mental.

Illness is nothing more than their poor diet; you are what you eat, at any energy level.

Most of the time, everything happens unconsciously, mechanically, and, when you succeed in bringing to the light of consciousness some discomforts, perhaps untreated wounds from your childhood, you do not always want or can heal them.

So, what do you do? You push them back into a corner of your mind, move on with your life, and pretend nothing has happened.

And sometimes someone forgets about it for a certain period of time. However, these unchanged emotions linger inside your Heart like lead weights; they gain strength and pull you down into depression, attracting situations, and people who will resonate with this discomfort.

If all this is ignored for a long time, the pain will manifest itself in the form of physical or mental illness of great importance.

You cannot run away from yourself; you are called to the Presence."

ME, "Yes, I know I still have a lot of pain inside of me to deal with. Starting from my birth, when my mother died giving birth to me.

And I also know that my cancer that appeared at the same age as her passing is no coincidence.

But I had no idea that even this pain of loss had been working in me constantly for all these years."

G.A, "It would have been impossible for you to bring the memory of your birth to consciousness, but this emotional pain came back to you in other forms, through other people, but you had no eyes to see the truth.

Now you cannot ignore it anymore."

ME, "Now I am scared and angry."

G.A, "I can feel it, and this condition is now more severe. But if you pay attention most of the time, all of you live in constant fear from your birth to your death.

Of course, you often experience discomfort unconsciously, but this is why you do most of your things; you act and make choices, whether you like it or not, always gripped with fear.

You are afraid of abandonment, of being alone, of not being loved enough, and therefore of not being accepted by the community.

You feel separated from your origin family, and you do not feel the unconditional love that surrounds you.

One of the worst evils of this era, the cancer that you are dealing with arises above all from this painful sense of separation from the rest of humanity, the Creator, and the fear that derives from it.

This state of affairs becomes a normal state of life, a normal thought pattern, and as you know, everything we believe in manifests itself in reality.

Not feeling well produces physical needs that, over time, become real addictions."

ME, "Like alcohol, smoking, and drugs?"

G.A, "Yes, but you already know their devastating consequences on your body.

At a lesser level, it starts with food.

A constant state of anxiety and dissatisfaction leads to the demand for greater quantities of food. And of course, you do not fill your stomach with vegetable-based meals but junk food, that is to say, refined fats and sugars.

So the poison that is introduced into your body every day, even if it does not kill you immediately, causes serious and irreparable damage, both in the body and mind."

ME, "But some people pay attention to what they eat, and yet they get sick anyway."

G.A, "As I told you before, you feed on different levels, and if you pay attention to what you eat and not what you think, the damage is done anyway.

Every day, falsified and selfish thoughts towards other people will cause illness. But what is worse is that some of these thoughts are considered normal by the mass, but this is not like that."

ME, "Which ones?"

G.A, "When you believe it is right to take advantage, even just for fun, from someone else's difficulties, for example for competition, or when you want to excel on the others putting in a bad light their work.

Often, you do it without realizing it, always motivated by fear, until sometimes the competition, the aggressive cheering in your stadiums becomes hatred for others.

You carry on this behavior until you experience a tragic episode, as your newscast reports regularly, or you get sick.

Only then, there is a moment of awakening in you, you realize with horror, thanks to the pain, what you have done or, if you get sick, you ask yourself; why me?"

Chapter 2: Acceptance or Resignation

"Diseases of the soul are more dangerous

than those of the body."

Cicero

ME, "When the damage is done, do we have to resign to our fate and regret our inability to see how things really stand?"

G.A, "Nobody talks about resignation, which is an aggressive feeling towards ourselves.

If anything, I recommend the acceptance for what is because it gives the possibility, through pain and observation, to grow and evolve spiritually, mentally, and, lastly, to heal.

Emotional pain, although unbearable, can be managed and become a valuable tool for entering a state of deep Presence.

Also, use feelings such as anger, hatred, fear to stay in the present moment without letting you drag and drown in a raging sea of emotions, stay there, and observe them without judgment.

Is the disease attracted to you? The answer is yes, like any other things, people, and events in your life.

Someone, in this context, speaks of Karma, but the fact of the matter does not change; if we understand Karma as a law of cause and effect, it, therefore, has the same nature as the Law of Attraction.

Everything moving within you is translated outside, into manifested reality, into action, and consequences of such actions.

Accepting what you are not able to change allows you to overcome the worst part of the situation you are experiencing."

ME, "We are constantly threatened by the feeling of fear in what we think, say, and do.

But once done, if we realize it, can we immediately run for cover and avoid the occurrence of the disease in the future?"

G.A, "Yes, and no.

If you realize you have a recurring thought of fear about, for example, getting sick, you should know the nature of this thought and how long it has been living within you.

Fear is one of the most powerful emotions and attracts like a magnet what you do not want to experience; it greatly increases the possibility of unpleasant events in your reality.

You do not always realize that things work like this because the manifestation of the situations you think of, maybe takes years to become real, but at that point, going from a negative thought to another, you have forgotten about it.

You forgot the unconscious request addressed, despite yourself to the Universe, but it gave you back in solid form what you created with the energy-thought and energy-emotion.

However, if you realize you have negative thoughts and emotions in time, the damage can be limited and even a lot.

The constant expectation of a healthy life counterbalances the fear of disease, and the cleaning of negative thought through powerful feelings, such as Acceptance and Faith, change it and make it harmless forever.

After all, Love is much more powerful than fear. "

ME, "Does Acceptance for medicine-recommended heavy therapies also help strengthen their healing effect?"

G.A, "Each healing process is preceded by an act of Love and Compassion towards yourself, whether you are aware of it or not.

It may be resignation in the beginning, but if you want to heal, it must give way to a higher emotion, namely Acceptance, as I said before.

Any necessary therapy should be welcomed in your Heart to be effective, and you should nourish with it, just like you do with a healthy meal.

Talk lovingly to your body, like a child, explain to it that you will be there at any time and that you will support it throughout the treatment.

Feed it with Love and Conscious Attention.

This will help accepting even the hardest of therapies because it will know it is never alone and loved.

In a body where there is no more anger, the medicine works better."

Although his words gave me feelings of peace and serenity, I realized that fear for the future was still in my heart. My path in the fight against cancer had just begun, and the only sure thing was that I wanted to experience it in full awareness, whatever happened.

I could not change the causes that led me to this experience, but I could choose how to walk the path towards healing.

I felt close to all those people who, like me, were in the trenches with weapons in hand, ready for the war against cancer, so I decided that every time, from that day on, I felt strong, I would share my strength with them.

Now, I had an extra responsibility.

But I had to start from the beginning and face my suffering.

Chapter 3: Suffering in the Healing Process

"Illness, involuntary access to ourselves, enslaves us to depth,

it condemns us to it.

The patient?

A metaphysician, despite himself."

Emil Cioran

Nothing is more difficult than making decisions and then taking full responsibility for your life.

It is the first lesson of the Law of Attraction.

Everything starts from here.

Even a recovery path from any disease makes no difference, regardless of how painful it can be.

Dealing with physical pain and emotional suffering is never easy, but what you get from this work is a precious gift that no one can ever steal from us, even after death.

When my Angel talked about the meaning of pain in the journey of life, I felt comforted and loved because I could perceive the love of the Creator even through the difficult trials that life put before me.

G.A, "Pain must never be rejected but observed in a state of full Presence, and so must all the emotions that cause it, such as anger, fear, or loneliness.

These feelings are the root from which several diseases originate or from which suffering events arise in your life.

But pain can be used to fully understand, by staying in the present moment, to face your aspects that need to be changed from negative to positive.

The Law of Attraction has placed them before you, like a mirror, so that you can identify everything that has caused this state of affairs.

It is not a punishment, but an opportunity if you do not be overwhelmed by events and try to have eyes to see."

ME, "But when you suffer a lot, your mind is almost in shock, and you can hardly contain it. Mental images of fear then translate into words and actions that never lead to anything good. "

G.A, "So, more damage is added.

This is why it is necessary, even in these conditions, to remain in a state of Presence; here, the pain is greatly reduced, the Soul is in a situation of peace and Love, and it can slowly regain control over the mind and inner clarity.

Suffering is turned into a compassionate Presence for yourself and the pain of others, and you feel more and more strengthened and ready to face the challenges of life.

This is the only way to suffer less and less and make it bear fruit."

ME, "It would be better to train to the Presence when you are not at the height of a painful moment.

In my experience, whenever I suffer, I fall prey to my negative thoughts for a long time, which causes negative emotions and also physical discomforts, such as a stomachache or headache. It often happens to many people to somatize inner states of malaise into health problems."

G.A, "You can always awaken and contribute to the healing process, as well as to protect yourself from painful relapses of the disease.

But it is necessary to remain in a state of balance between the body, mind, and soul.

Many therapists recommend monitoring your thoughts to change them if they are dysfunctional, but this is tough work if you do not strengthen yourself in the state of Presence first.

To answer your question, staying alert and aware when you are not facing a painful path certainly helps you to be stronger and master of your thoughts in dark times.

Everyone has their own time, and everyone is called to do their best in this regard.

Always remember that the effort you make to stay centered is important to reach the final result; it is thus possible to realize that everything you resist for the Law of Attraction is strengthened and concretely manifested in your reality.

The less Beauty you can see within yourself, the less you can understand the world you live in.

Your Heart becomes harsh and closes, and you need to live painful experiences again and again to reopen it.

But this vicious circle can be interrupted if you immediately put an end to criticism and complaint in your thoughts and words."

Chapter 4: Health and Wellness as a Choice

"To heal is to touch with love that which was previously touched by fear."
Stephen Levine

ME, "We criticize and complain almost without realizing it. And we do not see the damage we do to ourselves and others."

G.A, "It is exactly like this.

If you were already aware of the responsibility you have not only towards yourself but the people around you, you would probably be more careful in expressing judgments and complaining.

When you focus on the flaws of others, attracting that type of energy, you are actually creating sickness, different kinds of pain, accidents, and so on.

With judgment, the heart hardens, and you become blind and resentful, and you start manifesting bad life experiences.

If you do not realize it and regain control of yourself, you create a near-future of pain and disease.

On the contrary, deciding to stop complaining can immediately produce miracles in your existence.

It is enough one week without complaints, and you will start living incredible experiences also from the health point of view."

ME, "A kind of self-healing?"

G.A, "Mostly, it is a profound, conscious choice that leads to healing and staying healthy.

Even your quantum physics has proved the existence of the Law of Attraction because it states that the observer's act brings an intention from the invisible realm to that of tangible matter.

The inner will is the engine of everything and is made even more powerful in the act of realizing, so what you believe about your health becomes real.

Many Individuals of Light have always tried to convey this message to you that is the basis of life itself; its understanding opens the door to an integral Life, free of disease and poverty because it is founded on Love and Oneness with the Whole.

Your medicine, both traditional and holistic, is a great help in the healing process and in keeping you healthy, but it can do nothing if you do not decide to change your vibrational frequency."

ME, "What do you mean by changing the vibrational frequency?"

G.A, "To mean that the way you think, speak, and act determines the way your cells talk to each other. So if you keep choosing criticism, judgment, and complaining, the information contained in your cells degrades to a low level of energy, and this makes them vulnerable to diseases.

Have you ever heard of Epigenetics?"

ME, "Yes, I have. It is a branch of molecular biology that studies genetic mutations that do not directly depend on the original DNA of a person, but on his lifestyle, that is, on what he eats, the environment in which he lives, and so on."

G.A, "Exactly, but DNA is also influenced by what the individual thinks, by his or her deepest feelings.

Because it is on his intimate emotions, whether good or bad, that his every decision depends; from food to the choice of his lifestyle.

Soul brands matter, not the opposite.

If you choose to live a life of health and well-being, even if you are facing challenging treatments following an illness, bring attention to your Heart, stay alert, and train yourself not to criticize or complain.

At first, it will not be easy because you will think about them automatically, but try to refrain and, after a while, you will see that rather than complaining, you will say benevolent words of gratitude towards yourself and others.

Miracles are always an act of manifested love, and healing through the choice of treatments right for you is always a miracle, and you have the ability to make it happen.

So make the decision every day to live healthily and take full responsibility for it; begin right away, whether you are healing or feeling well.

Use the wonderful tool of creative visualization and recall to you with thoughts and words the state of health worthy of the Children of the Creator, and feel this Love within.

Make it a shield against any intrusion of evil and its temptations, and keep yourselves honest in the Heart."

There was no greater feeling of Love than the one aroused within me after a conversation with my Divine Guide. After talking with him, everything became clearer and more feasible, even if he had never hidden me the effort of this journey towards my physical and emotional health regaining.
I knew that I would have to work hard, but I also knew that if I had chosen well, I would not be alone but supported and protected by all the love in the world.

Chapter 5: All-Around Therapies

"People can recover from the disease,

diseases can make people recover."

Gerhard Uhlenbruck

So, I began my journey towards recovery, and at the same time, the chemotherapy cycles.

It was not easy at all.

But I did not expect it to be.

So, armed with courage and patience after the first treatment, I accepted the hair loss.

And this was not easy at all too.

However, I specialized in the choice of colored scarves and complicated turbans since wigs were not for me, so I continued the path, always asking for the support of my Guardian Angel.

I decided to develop with him a series of effective therapies to be combined with chemotherapy so that it would be enhanced and its side-effects greatly reduced.

So one day, I asked him, "How about combining other types of treatments to enhance this cure? Do you have any suggestions?"

G.A, "Whatever you decide to undertake, you must always start with what suits you best.

What makes you happy and gives you well-being?

An answer to this question is necessary before starting.

However, going down into your Heart to find centering is important to have a clear vision of yourself and the situation you are experiencing.

I can give you anyway some basic tips, procedures that are good for anyone.

One of them is remembering to breathe.

I know it sounds ridiculous, but if you rest on your way to ingesting air, you will find out that you always do it in a rush and with all your muscles contracted.

This causes poor oxygenation of the blood and a consequent accumulation of toxins throughout your body. Toxins that, over time, produce mental and physical damage.

So remember yourself and your breath several times during the day, relax your body, and become aware of the air that enters and leaves your nostrils, distributes from the lungs to the blood and all the other organs of the body, invigorates and heals them, breath by breath.

The mind calms down and becomes clearer, and immediately a generalized state of well-being spreads within you, starting from you to the outside as a blessing and returns to you healthier than before.

Get the habit of breathing.

The correct breathing can be followed by a meditation session for those who already practice it or find it interesting to learn.

It does not need to last long, even ten minutes is enough; what matters is that it helps you reconnect with yourself, create well-being, and keep it over time.

ME, "The more we feel good, in harmony with ourselves, the better our choices will be, not only during medical treatment but also later, once the therapeutic path is finished."

G.A, "Exactly. But it is not automatic for everyone.

There are people who, after bad bronchopneumonia just recovered, resume smoking cigarettes as and more than before.

Up to the experience of lung cancer, from which, it is not certain, they can recover.

Or people with serious cases of gastritis and perforating ulcers, who do not want to follow a diet that protects them from dangerous relapses.

As long as you have enough suffering, you hit the bottom of physical and mental pain.

Then the time for the choice that leads to healing or to permanently leave the earthly life comes.

On the contrary, when you decide for conscious work on yourself, many habits change, even the food-related ones.

Because you are also what you eat.

Starting with the preparation of meals which should never be done in a hurry and distractedly, but with love and attention, so that every molecule of each food you will ingest, is by resonance, in harmony with your thoughts and emotions.

So, if you bless and love the food you prepare and eat, alone or with your loved ones, it will be imbued with these powerful feelings, and once ingested, it will heal or protect your body from disease.

What starts from you comes back to you."

ME, "Do we have to pay attention to our emotions because they always implement the Law of Attraction?"

G.A, "The Law of Attraction always works for good or bad, it is neutral.

But if you know its mechanism, it is easier to attract joy rather than pain, health rather than disease.

And it is an efficient tool for healing when you are aware."

Chapter 6: Love, Gratitude, and Forgiveness

"Saying thank you creates love."

Daphne Rose Kingma

"The most difficult forgiveness is the one that a man must find in himself."

Anonymous

ME, "Living a stressful life in our cities and always in a hurry, it is difficult to think of never getting sick."

G.A, "You remember yourself the moment that Life, in its immense wisdom, decides to awaken you from your frenzy; if in this case, a serious illness occurs, it is because all the previous signals have been ignored.

What you now call stress in the past was known by other names, but it has always existed and made life very hard and heavy.

The accumulation of stress, therefore, is inevitable, and when it reaches unacceptable levels and is not adequately counterbalanced, it becomes one of the primary causes of diseases. And it is precisely in these moments that you realize the need to run for cover, to change.

Illness is always a message of urgency from the Soul that calls for a radical change, an alarm bell that if you continue to ignore, it will no longer have a resolution in this life.

So, I push you not to despair, whatever your health condition, to gently approach this experience with Love, ready to fight every illness with an open Heart but fully accepting reality for what it is.

Rejection of the present moment is an act of madness, and you cannot afford it.

You have to be clear-headed to face the challenge.

Only in this condition of total integrity, you can start forgiving yourself and take your responsibilities to reshape the mental and emotional mechanisms that have brought you this far."

ME, "A challenge within the challenge."

G.A, "Exactly. It is not impossible but challenging, especially in the moment of physical suffering.

If you can face the disease not with shame but as a possibility for growth, then you will develop unconditional gratitude towards every aspect of your life.

This same gratitude will be a primary source of protection against any other disease because one of the most evident effects is the strengthening of your immune system."

ME, "How?"

G.A, "Love, Forgiveness, and Gratitude act directly on strengthening the immune defenses that prevent you from developing diseases.

Spirit forges matter, never the opposite, even if some of your scientists declare the opposite.

Get used to feeling Gratitude, observing the reality that surrounds you with Love, and changing any worry into Forgiveness."

ME, "There is a lot to forgive then. But how long does it take to get into the healthy habit of thanking from the morning as soon as you wake up and forgiving instead of criticizing and judging ourselves and others?"

G.A, "It takes perseverance and firm will to insert a new practice into the daily routine, replacing a bad habit that only damages, with a new one that immediately fills the Heart with Joy.

You must have the courage to become *addict* to this joy until you completely depend on it; Gratitude must be the first thought in the morning and the last before going to sleep.

This is an authentic act of Love towards oneself and the rest of the world.

A mind and a heart educated in Love, Gratitude, and Forgiveness protect the body from any disease and make the human being aware and happy.

There will come a time in your schools when it will be understood the need to train young learners from these three Higher emotions, and they will be the basic virtues and skills of your new leaders."

ME, "When I think I learned to forgive, I realize that I did not forget the evil suffered. And I think I failed."

G.A, "Complete Forgiveness is not forgetfulness, or the wrong suffered, and the resulting pain could not be processed.

Your responsibility attracts you not to run away from the traumatic memories that damaged you, but to face them with awareness, thus avoiding living in a spiral of hatred and pain that would lead you to repeat, pouring out on others, the evil suffered in the past.

If you bring Attention and Love to memories where there is still resentment, you will no longer be held hostage to your past, prisoners of the pain that still burns, but you will be healed and free."

Final Remarks

"Never fear shadows. They simply mean there's a light
Shining somewhere nearby."
Ruth E. Renkel

We have been taught that illness is a misfortune, but I discovered, also thanks to my personal journey, that, as with all life events, it is our personal (albeit unconscious) creation.

When a condition of imbalance is established within us for more or less long periods, whether we realize it or not, we lay the foundations for the experience of a disease.

There is discomfort within us, a crisis that we have to face, despite ourselves, through a disease that we did not expect to discover, and that scares the hell.

But if we get to understand that due to the effect of the Law of Attraction, we encouraged this disease into our existence, thanks to the same law, we can decide to attract the right situations, people, and treatments to heal and never get sick again.

If we learn to perceive this experience as a gift or an opportunity for growth, we can stimulate the change of our way of being.

Illness requires us to stop and listen carefully, to examine the many aspects of our life that we no longer like, that bother us, and that must be deleted to make room for new values and new priorities.

The path is hard, but we always have all the aids we need to heal if we are sick and to keep ourselves healthy in full respect and love for our body, mind, and soul.

Today I am cured, even if traditional medicine is keen to stress that relapses may recur even after many years, so it is very cautious in considering me *out of the woods.*

However, what matters is how I feel, what thoughts and emotions I want to feel, and how I choose to communicate them because I realized the extraordinary power we have that allows us to fulfill our personal paradise on Earth.

I realized that the responsibility to stay healthy is not only towards ourselves but also towards those who love us and who care about our well-being and happiness. Therefore, if we do not take care of our physical and mental health, risking to get sick, we harm not only ourselves but also cause deep suffering to them.

The choice is not obvious, but to be true, it must be aware.

One evening, after a busy day spent mostly in the hospital, I felt tired and unmotivated, and there was still a long way to go... I could only think *"why?"*

G.A, "Each path must come to its end, and the darkest pain creates a knowledge that will enrich your soul forever.

Do not fear anything because you are never alone.

My Strength is your Strength; my Love is His Love for you and for all creatures who, through suffering, open their Heart to a new Truth.

The time of pain is running out, and it will give way to a new awareness; you are the creators of your reality.

Love, Well-being, and Prosperity have never been denied to you and never will be; you have to perceive them and open your Heart.

And now you know how to do it."

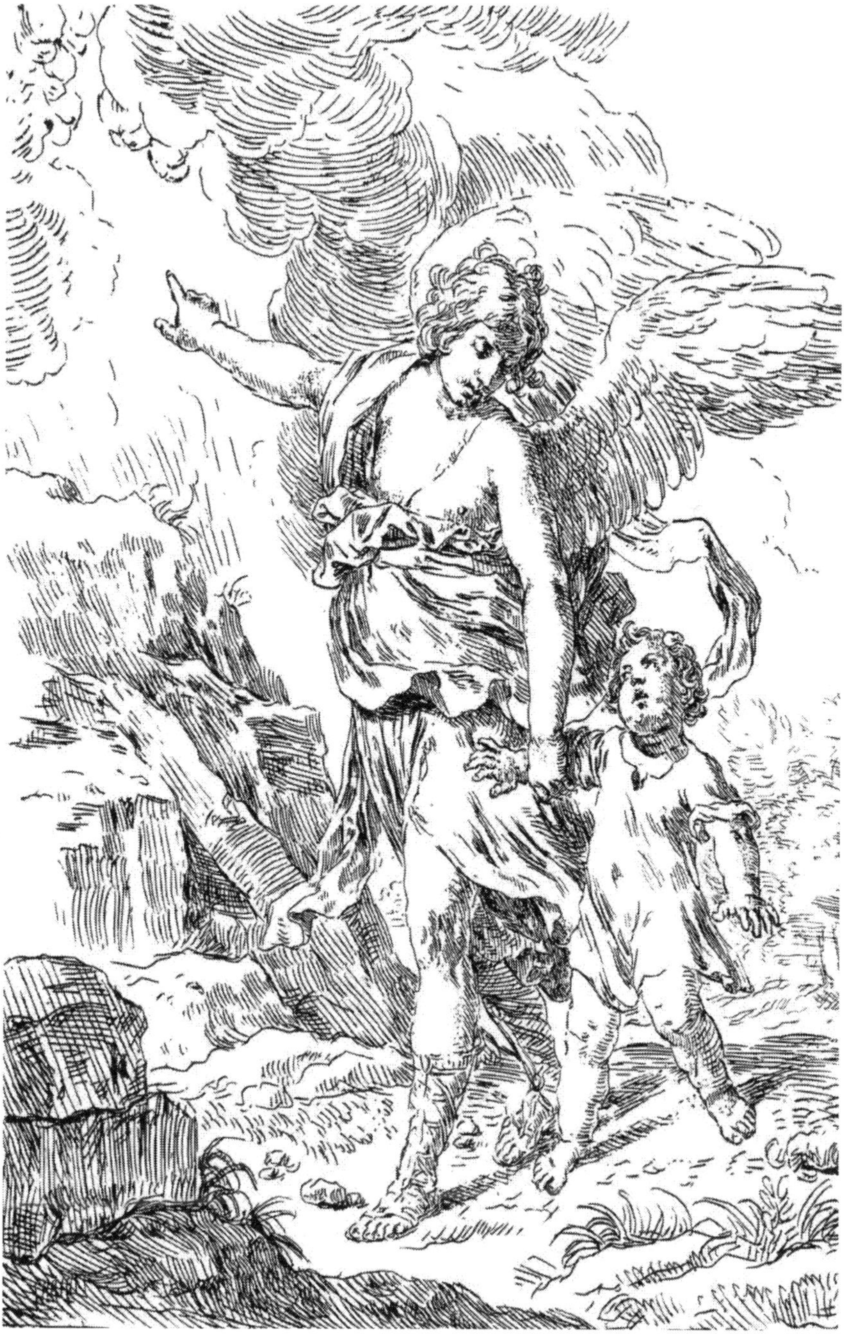

Conclusion to the Collection

He who uses clay pots as if they were silver is great,

but he who uses silver pots as if they were clay is no less.

A weak soul cannot bear wealth.

Seneca

So, we have reached the end of this first part of the journey.

Now looking back, you can see the memory of yourself as you were before, lost in the external world, and with a constant fear of failure. You find yourself experiencing the limitless possibilities of your existence.

You feel that you have the world at your feet, an Open Heart, and broader consciousness. You can now accumulate wealth and abundance without being blamed for being visionaries or materialists.

You have learned to set aside the judgment towards the world, to have Faith, and to touch the results of this Faith, which is no longer blind because now you have eyes to see.

Do not be unprepared to external events and do not give in despair; you are no longer part of the ranks of whiny, that is, of those who blame their own misfortunes to external causes.

Keep within you the bud of the new life, the one you have always dreamed of, keeping intact the understanding and compassion for those who are not ready to start the journey yet because everything is already perfect like this, and the judgment does not touch you like before.

Now, begin to catch the *essence* beyond the *form* because you can see Abundance, Prosperity, Perfection, and Love around you, perceiving that Well-being and Wealth are at hand.

Everything else is a pure illusion, a reflection of our consciousness.

But there is still a lot to discover and to know.

The journey is still long and full of wonders.

And I will share it with you.

With Love.

Printed in Great Britain
by Amazon